The Dancer Prepares

Clockwise from upper left: Isadora
Duncan, Ruth St. Denis, Mary Wig-
man, Doris Humphrey and Charles
Weidman, Martha Graham, and Ted
Shawn. Photographs from The Library
& Museum of the Performing Arts,
The New York Public Library at
Lincoln Center

Second Edition

The Dancer Prepares

MODERN DANCE FOR BEGINNERS

James Penrod
Janice Gudde Plastino
UNIVERSITY OF CALIFORNIA, IRVINE

Illustrations by Robert Carr

MAYFIELD PUBLISHING COMPANY

Library of Congress Catalog Card Number: 79-91836
International Standard Book Number: 0-87484-340-5

Manufactured in the United States of America
Mayfield Publishing Company
285 Hamilton Avenue, Palo Alto, California 94301

This book was set in Sabon and Helvetica Light by Acme Type Company and was printed and bound by the George Banta Company. Spon-
soring editor was C. Lansing Hays, Maggie Cutler supervised editing,
and Carol King was manuscript editor. Book design by Nancy Sears.
Michelle Hogan supervised production. Cover by Mary Burkhardt.

Contents

Preface

Movement never lies. Everything that a
dancer does on the stage tells the audience
what he is.
— Martha Graham

This book is written for you who are taking your first course in modern dance to introduce you to the content of the course and to explain your role as a student. The authors assume you have little or no background in the art or technique of the dance.

No one can be taught how to be an artist, but you can be taught the craft of an art form. We hope to help you discover a new appreciation of the arts in general and to inspire in you a desire for self-discovery, self-discipline, and eventually self-expression in the art form of dance. This book introduces you to such rudiments of the dancer's craft as basic techniques, dance clothes, and the care of your body. It also discusses choreographic fundamentals and evaluation procedures. We hope these objective principles will help you to form a subjective ideal that will inspire you to commit yourself more fully to the dance world.

It is of little consequence why you have decided to study modern dance. The important thing is that you have enrolled in a course to learn the most exciting of the movement forms. You have chosen a course that is physically rigorous and exhausting, mentally stimulating and exasperating, and creatively exciting and frustrating. It is probably one of the most self-satisfying courses that you will take. We do not assume that you will become a professional dancer, although we have directed the ideas in this book toward that goal. We do, however, hope you will experience the joy of movement well-executed, the exhilaration of creative endeavor, and the appreciation of dance—the most fleeting of the art forms.

This book is primarily concerned with the analysis of modern dance techniques, combinations, and vocabulary. Although it is written for the beginning student, the book contains information that will be of value to the intermediate student as well.

The revised edition has been updated and expanded with practical and theoretical information that will increase the usefulness of the book. Chapter 3, "Technique Analysis," has additional material relating to the qualitative analysis of movement and movement phrases. Chapter 5, "History," includes additional references to pioneer and contemporary choreographers of modern dance. Chapter 6, "Choreographic Approaches," includes·exercises in body movement and movement sources and a further discussion of choreographic methods. Chapter 7, "Evaluation and Criticism," contains guidelines for observing and evaluating professional and nonprofessional performances and choreography.

We do not intend to preach a philosophy or theory of some ephemeral art form that can be mastered by reading statements about how to dance. We do intend to deal with concrete, specific, practical matters relating to the mastery of the creative and technical aspects of dance.

Values

Chapter 1

Love the art in yourself, rather than
yourself in art.
— Stanislavsky

If you have signed up for your first modern dance class, which might be called something like Modern, Contemporary, Creative, Freestyle, Dance 40A, or PE 5B, you may be wondering just what modern dance is.

DEFINING MODERN DANCE

In the past, "modern dance" represented the viewpoints and movement concepts of each of several dancers or choreographers. For example, there was the particular modern dance technique of Martha Graham, of Doris Humphrey, or of Mary Wigman. As the horizons of the dance artists have widened, the various movement forms have become more alike. In the past, it was easy to recognize ballet by its codified positions and movements. This is no longer true. Today many "ballet" choreographers utilize the movement concepts of the modern dancer, and many of the body placements and exercises of the ballet dancer are now used in the "modern" techniques. Many choreographers now include in their work not only the elusive modern dance techniques, but also the principles of jazz, ballet, and ethnic dance.

A Blend of Techniques

If the term "modern dance" were to be defined for today, it should be broad enough to include all the diverse approaches existing now and likely to exist in the future.

Rather than a concise definition of what modern dance is, perhaps more important to you is what it can contribute to the enrichment of your life. It can help keep your body trim, give a grace and poise to all your movements, and contribute to your general sense of well-being through the

What Dance Can Do for You

pleasure of a well-toned body. It can introduce you to a new form in which you experience the joy of movement and compete solely with yourself. It can heighten your appreciation of music, the plastic arts, and all movement forms. It can increase your respect and understanding of the dancer's profession. And, finally, a modern dance course will expand your awareness and appreciation of the way you and others move.

DANCE AS
A CAREER

It is hoped that some of you will be inspired enough by your modern dance experience to choose dance as a professional career. Dedication to the art of the dance *might* require you to forsake money, fame, and even family in order to reach the pinnacle of artistic success in the dance world. Many sacrifices are involved in such an aspiration, often without the longed-far rewards. After five to ten years of dedicated work, you may not yet be accepted into a dance company. Even if you are accepted, the company may be unable to pay you a living wage. You must often be prepared to support yourself by means other than dancing. Because the financial rewards are so low, living conditions may be barely adequate and certainly not luxurious. The hardships of giving concerts or arranging performances of your own works can be heartbreaking as well as rewarding.

Yet under such trying circumstances the art of dance flourishes. Dedicated, disciplined people continue to expand the vocabulary of movement. New forms are continually created in the artist's push forward. The hope of making a contribution to the understanding of life keeps the search alive.

Perhaps dance does not appeal to you on that level. Perhaps you have seen the beautiful women and handsome men, dressed in the latest fashions, who dance across television or movie screens. Such "Hollywood dreams" are within the realm of possibility. But you must decide whether you are willing to make the commitment necessary to attain them.

There have been and will continue to be those few dancers who have extraordinary luck and who obtain a good job without too much hard work. This happens rarely and in the long run usually has disastrous results. Almost always, these dancers fail because an inadequate background and bad training have not prepared them for the next job. It is risky to let yourself be talked into a job before you are ready. If your training is to be interrupted or stopped by a job, then think twice before you take that job. Performing experience should be a part of your dance education, but it should supplement training, not take the place of it.

Anyone who is dedicated to a dance career must be prepared to work and work hard. You probably will perform before you have had five years of training, but you should continue to return to the classroom to keep your body in top condition. If you become a dancer, your body will be your working instrument, just as a violin is a violinist's instrument. Unlike the violinist, however, the dancer must build the instrument while learning technique and the skills needed to perform.

Like an Olympic athlete, the dancer should be dedicated to acquiring the greatest skills possible—not for financial gain or simply to win, but for the satisfaction of giving your best. No less than a devoted athlete, the dancer must be disciplined and dedicated to such a high purpose.

DANCE FOR VIEWING

As a dance student, you should attend dance concerts to see the finished product that was started in the studio. It is often impossible to see a professional performance unless you are living in a large city or near a university that sponsors touring companies. The alternative is to see professional performances on film and television. Many excellent films of dance exist and can be ordered for a small fee. Commercial television seldom offers first-rate concert dance, but it does offer entertaining dance by exciting, competent performers and choreographers. Educational and public television often show new works as well as older works of leading choreographers. Many universities have fine companies or Orchesis groups—Orchesis is a national collegiate dance group with individual chapters on a number of campuses—who do exciting, creative productions. It is to your advantage as a student to see dance, whether good or bad. You can always learn something at a dance concert, even if it is only something not to do.

Dance Audiences

Interest in all forms of dance is rapidly growing in the United States, but the audience for modern dance has traditionally been smaller than audiences for other art forms. There are several reasons for this. One is that modern dance is a relatively new art. As opposed to opera and ballet,

4

which are often supported financially by an established society, modern dance is thought by many people to be only for other artists and dancers. This is unfortunate. Modern dance reflects the time in which it is danced. It is usually contemporary, because it is created by and for those who are interested in the reflection of life today.

Another reason modern dance has not enjoyed a wide following is the stigma that formerly existed upon using the human body as a medium for art. The Puritan influence fostered the belief that the sinful body should be hidden from view; only the mind and soul were worthy of serious study. More recently, the human body has become more acceptable as an appropriate medium for artistic expression. The belief that dancing bodies are sinful now exists only in certain sections of our society, and even there this view is changing.

Audiences and Finances

Many modern dance artists and their companies are beginning to enjoy limited financial support as they become acceptable to the general public. One artist who has done a great deal to promote the acceptance of modern dance is Martha Graham. Her success came slowly, only after many years of work and dedication. She achieved her greatest success as a performer and choreographer in the late 1960s in her seventh decade. Graham retired as a dancer in 1969.

But even such famous artists as Martha Graham cannot maintain their companies on audience support alone. Most of the established professional companies are forced to rely on private foundation money or government grants. Stipulations are sometimes imposed on the person who accepts these funds. These demands may hinder or help the artist. It would be to everybody's advantage if the companies could be supported by the audiences who attend the performances.

Certainly the size of an audience is not always the best measure of the quality of a work of art. Artists are often ahead of their times. One criterion of the caliber of the artist is the ability to see new trends and to synthesize these insights in a new way. Therefore works of art may not evoke a response from people who have not been introduced to the situation as the artist has interpreted it.

Like the centuries of dancers who have gone before, you are embarking on one of the most exciting experiences of a lifetime. Even if your dance training consists of one course only, you will be awakened to an unlimited range of body movements. You will dance about those things that concern all people everywhere. These things are the search for an awareness of what it means to be alive, to create, and to begin to understand humankind and our place in the universe.

Preparation

Chapter 2

The human body is an instrument for the production of art in the life of the human soul.
— Alfred North Whitehead

After signing for a modern dance class, you might be asking —as many students do—a series of questions. What should I wear? How should I wear it? What happens in a dance class? How much do I need to know about music? All are good questions, and the answers will help you get the most out of your classroom experience.

This chapter provides general answers. To learn the special requirements of your course, check with your teacher or a representative of the class. Some teachers like to use the first class meeting as a discussion period, and you should find out whether ordinary clothes or dance clothes should be worn to the first session. If there are any unanswered questions in your mind, ask! Most teachers are used to answering questions and are happy to help.

CLOTHING
Special
Requirements

Often the beginning dance student wonders why in most dance studios students are asked to wear special form-fitting clothes for the dance class, clothing that could be thought of as an outer skin. There are several reasons.

Dance is a visual art that uses the dancer's body to create architectural designs in space. Any clothing that does not conform to the outline of the body will alter the designs created in that space. Some students might ask if this isn't desirable in some cases. The answer would be an emphatic Yes. Clothing can evoke an era, enhance some movements, and give a new look to the movement and the spatial design that a silhouetted body alone could never achieve. Students in a basic technique class, however, are not usually concerned with these problems, unless they are experimenting to find new movements inherent in the restrictions imposed by the costume.

The second reason for special clothing is that the main concern of classroom technique is to align your body in a series of exercises that will strengthen and stretch it in order to make it responsive to the physical demands that will be made upon it. The teacher must be able to see the placement of your body in order to give an intelligent criticism of your work. Guessing as to what you might be doing under piles of clothing is dangerous! Faulty placement of your body in exercises will weaken and even injure you if you repeat it often enough. You could compare an overdressed dancer to a building that is covered with unnecessary exterior frills that hide its basic structure.

Dance clothing also puts one in the proper frame of mind to work in the dance class. A person usually associates certain activities with a certain kind of clothing. For example, when you swim, you wear a bathing suit. Clothing that restricts movement prevents proper exercising, in the same way that ordinary clothing would restrict the movement of a swimmer in the water. When you are dressed in clothes worn only while dancing, you soon associate the clothing with dancing, which, in turn, helps put you in the mood of the experience to come.

Today's simple dance costume has evolved over many centuries. The first dance costumes were styled after the clothing worn everyday by the dancers in the courts of the sixteenth century. The women wore long, full dresses that hid their bodies and prevented freedom of movement. As time passed and more technical demands were made on the women dancers, their dresses were shortened to permit freer movement. Men's costumes also were simplified until finally a simple leotard was introduced by Jules Léotard, a famous French acrobat, in the mid-nineteenth century. At last dancers could appear without voluminous piles of cloth that restricted and hid movement.

In the ballet, women eventually wore the long "romantic" skirts or the short "classical" skirts that we associate with the "white" ballet today. They also wore toe shoes that allowed them to rise onto the tips of their toes to evoke an ethereal, romantic quality in their movements. The modern dancers broke with this tradition to use simple tights and leotards or free-flowing gowns and bare feet that allow more freedom of movement.

Sometimes students or their parents think the wearing of dancer's tights is immoral. Consider the clothing worn on the street today! Tights are modest by comparison.

Most dance schools require special clothing. This clothing can be purchased in dance boutiques or department stores. Check with your teacher before purchasing shoes, tights, or leotards. If the teacher requests shoes, these can be ballet slippers or a modern slipper that leaves the toes and heels exposed. Most modern dancers do not wear shoes while dancing.

Women's Clothing Women usually wear tights which cover the legs and hips and a leotard worn under or over these which covers the hips and trunk. If tights are seamed, the seam is worn in the back. Panties or a girdle may be worn under the tights but under no circumstances must these garments be allowed to show. The showing of the outline of the panty beneath the leotard destroys the long look of the leg. If you feel uncomfortable without panties, perhaps a brief bikini panty will suffice. A well-fitting bra should be worn by anyone with a breast size above 32A. Breast tissue can be torn away from the underlying musculature if the breasts are not properly supported.

Stirrup tights are preferred, although some dancers still choose tights with feet cut off at the ankle or opened along the sole. The latter can also be worn for other types of dance classes that require shoes.

With the popularization and purchase of dancewear by the general public, many styles of leotards in many new materials have become available. Dancers seem to delight in finding different ways to wear the dance garments. The only rule to remember is that your body must be visually free and clean. Within this rule almost anything goes.

Mensturation is a natural body process which a woman experiences approximately 350 times in her life. If the dancer regards it as a natural phenomenon, it should cause no problems. She should take dance class with no hesitation during the menstrual period. If she feels sluggish or slightly uncomfortable, she will probably feel much better after the class. Often, stretching can relieve cramps. Even if she has pain associated with the onset of menstruation, she should not miss more than one class a month. It is too difficult to catch up in the class. It must be stressed that if the woman is contemplating dance as a career, it is not acceptable to miss class. There will be many times when she must audition or perform with cramps or other unpleasant sensations associated with the menstrual period. It is to her advantage to learn to work at such times.

Sometimes a student is embarrassed at having to wear a pad under a tight-fitting leotard. Perhaps an internal tampon would relieve her distress. The tampon is undetectable when in place and does not interfere with movement. It is painless to use and does not disturb the hymen (commonly known as the maidenhead). The use of a tampon is a matter of personal preference. The main consideration is to be comfortable and at ease during the menstrual period. Whatever helps a student to enjoy the dance class is acceptable.

Men's clothing consists of tights pulled up firmly in the crotch to avoid a baggy, droopy-drawers look. The tights are usually of a heavier material, less sheer than women's tights. The seams are worn in the back. A dance belt is worn under the tights to hold the genitals firmly in place and to help prevent ruptures. The one-piece dance belt, about the same size as jockey shorts, gives more support than the athletic supporter (jock-strap) which is ordinarily worn under gym clothes. The dance belt is designed to be worn with the wide cloth part in front. The dance belt is available in either black or white. The belt should be the same color as the tights so that it doesn't show through.

Men's Clothing

Tights should never hang down in the crotch and distort the body line, a fault that is a clear indication of a beginning student. Male dancers frequently hold the tights up with an ordinary belt around the waist, then roll the tights down over the belt. Others hold the tights up with clip-on suspenders or with elastic bands sewn onto the tights and carried over the shoulders as regular suspenders. The suspenders give a better line in that they eliminate the bulky belt line. A tight-fitting, waist-length T-shirt is worn over the torso. This can be tucked into the tights or hang out if it doesn't cover the pelvic area. For both men and women the tights and accessories should be worn so that the silhouette can be seen clearly.

Some dance schools allow dancers to wear gym shorts rather than invest in special clothing. The main drawback to shorts is that they do not protect your legs while you are doing floor work, and they do not keep the body heat concentrated in the legs, which helps to keep the muscles warm. They are also not as aesthetically pleasing to the body line as tights.

Clothing Variations

Tights and leotards are produced in many colors. Some schools insist on uniformity in the colors worn by the students. Check with your teacher before buying colors other than black (worn by both men and women) or pink (customarily reserved for the use of women). If you are allowed to choose your own colors, consider what colors do to the look of your body. If you want to make your body as attractive and slim-appearing as possible, black is for you. The darker colors make you look slimmer. Lighter colors are better on a slim body. If you wear colored tights, it is preferable to wear subdued tones. Remember that bright, garish colors tend to enlarge. The top and the bottom of the outfit should blend harmoniously. A severe contrast in colors tend to chop your body visually into two sections, which is generally not very flattering. Some dancers prefer to wear warm-up garments over their leotards and tights. Some teachers object to these layers of clothing because the line of the body is distorted. Check with your teacher before purchasing and wearing warm-up garments.

Care of Clothing

Dance clothing can be expensive, but it will last for years if properly cared for. Dance clothes should be laundered *after each wearing,* either in warm water alone or with soap and water, in order to prevent fading, rotting, and odor. They should not be stored in a locker when wet with perspiration. Tights sometimes develop runs, which should be sewn as soon as practicable in order to assure a longer life for the garment. In addition, good hygiene and common courtesy indicate a shower after each class.

PERSONAL APPEARANCE

Hair Styles

The hair for both men and women (when the hair styles are long) should be secured in such a way that it does not fall over your face or into your eyes. It is extremely distracting to the dancer and to the audience to have hair that insists on its own creative endeavors. You should find a hair style that is attractive and yet practical for dance.

Accessories

Before entering the classroom, you should check to see if you have with you all the accessories that might be needed: extra bobby pins, elastic bands for the hair (never for the shoes, as they break and present a physical hazard to everyone working), shoes if required, notebook and pencil if requested. If you perspire heavily, a towel is a good classroom accessory. For those who wear glasses, a strap to hold the glasses securely in place can be purchased at a sporting goods store. Since glasses are not worn in performance, some dancers purchase contact lenses.

Once the class work has begun, you should be prepared for any clothing emergency that might come up. It is very disturbing to the classroom continuity and to your concentration to be forced to leave the room or stop to adjust clothing. Preparation for such contingencies is the beginning of self-discipline.

Fully prepared, you put on the dance clothes and you walk into the studio to follow in the footsteps of a tradition that spans the centuries. It relates to the basic needs of the primitive tribesman, the courtier of the royal courts, and even the sophisticated disco dancer ecstatically moving to the pounding rhythm of the latest disco music.

CLASS PROCEDURES

As you walk into the studio you are quite likely to see a fairly large room with cylindrical wooden railings (called barres) attached to the walls. The dancer uses these to help balance while doing exercises. Some studios use a portable metal barre—others do not use barres at all. In the front of the room you might see a large mirror or series of mirrors covering one wall. The floor is usually of hardwood that gives slightly under the weight of the dancer's body, thereby preventing injuries and lessening fatigue. Many professional dancers refuse to dance on concrete. The floor should never be waxed or finished with a lacquer, as most gym floors are. The floor should be washed with water only—never a cleaning agent. Soaps leave a film that makes the floor slippery. The floor should be free of splinters, nails, and small holes.

Warm-up

As you look around you probably see people dressed in tights, some holding onto the barre, others seated on the floor, all warming up their bodies with simple movements before they begin more strenuous physical activity.

Numerous experiments have been conducted to determine whether or not a warm-up before other exercises has any value. The results of these experiments are contradictory and therefore inconclusive. Some test results state the warm-up was of great value in aiding the performance of athletes, others that there was no significant improvement. You should follow your teacher's own theories and methods of working.

As teachers for many years, we have found that the warm-up is valuable for three reasons: such exercise psychologically prepares you to start moving, increases the blood flow, and stimulates sluggish muscles.

Simple preparatory exercises could consist of rolling the head in a circle to warm the neck area, circling the shoulders to warm the chest area, slowly stretching upward, sideward, and forward to stretch out the whole body, relaxing the body in a forward slump and then returning to an upright position with tension to activate the reflexes, rolling or flexing the foot at the ankle to warm the ankle, and rising and descending slowly on the ball of the foot to stretch the gastrocnemius (calf muscle).

You should exercise caution about extreme stretching before your body is warmed up. Remember, start slowly and simply.

Accompaniment Then the teacher walks into the room, possibly accompanied by the pianist who will provide the music for the class. Some teachers use a hand drum to set the rhythm that you will dance to. Perhaps records will provide the accompaniment. The accompaniment will vary according to individual preference of the teacher and more often according to the financial backing of the department or school.

The teacher calls the class from their separate areas of the room, and thus begins your participation in the dance, which the philosopher Havelock Ellis in *The Dance of Life* calls "the source of all the arts that express themselves in the human person." In your new adventure you will explore the natural rhythms and physical movement possibilities of your body.

Every class has a basic rhythm or form to it. Often the class starts with the warm-up, then moves into the controlled exercises that strengthen your body and develop technique. Usually these exercises are preparing you to do some specific movements for the class on that day. Once you start the class, don't sit down, as your muscles get "cold" and you could needlessly injure yourself. Usually the exercises become more vigorous as the class progresses. Some teachers prefer to end the class with jumps or big movements, others prefer to work the class "down" with tranquil movements so that when you leave you are not as emotionally "high."

Some teachers use the barre in their exercises; others do not. Some teachers do exercises only on the floor or standing; others rarely use the floor. All methods and approaches are valid. All teachers are working toward the same goal, which can be attained in many ways—the goal of developing a beautiful and artistically expressive body for you.

The teacher will begin the class by demonstrating movement patterns for you to follow. Unless the teacher specifies that you are to do the movement in your own way, try to copy the teacher's way. An important part of dance training is to develop your "artistic eye" to see all the nuances of movement and then reproduce them as demonstrated. There are several reasons: correct execution of exercise is imperative if injuries are to be avoided and physical control is to be established; mastery of the body is part of the satisfaction that comes from dancing; and those who want to be professional dancers must learn movement patterns quickly and correctly. The dance world today is highly competitive and without large financial resources. The choreographer who must produce a work in a limited amount of time, sometimes as little as one week, is forced to hire well-qualified, well-trained dancers who learn quickly and correctly. Dancers who can do any movement required of them by the choreographer are usually hired first. You cannot learn to dance on the job.

Demonstrations

Sometimes the teacher, rather than demonstrating a movement pattern, will ask you to improvise movement. If asked to improvise, listen very carefully to the description that the teacher suggests as a basis for the movement. Don't try to intellectualize, plan the movement, or reproduce a movement that you have learned in the classroom. The chief value of improvisation is to free your body with movements that are natural to yourself, to encourage you to be spontaneous, and to stimulate your kinesthetic memory and imagination. Sometimes to stimulate the senses or the imagination, the teacher will ask you to recall a mood, a physical or emotional state of being, movement patterns in space and time, or to imagine how it would feel to be someone or something.

Improvisations

Many improvisational situations are available to the dancer and teacher. (Chapter 6 lists a number of them.) The possibilities are limited only by the limitations of the person who does them. If you can allow yourself to enter into the spirit of the improvisational experience, you will find it very rewarding. It may be the area of movement where you discover whether or not you want to be a dancer, teacher, or choreographer. Improvisation is a very important part of the modern dance experience, as important as the mastery of physical technique. Neither should be ignored. One trains the body, the other trains the spirit of the artist-to-be. The synthesis and mastery of the two make it possible to unite outer discipline and inner joy.

Attendance

Students usually know how to study in a regular academic class, but many are at a loss how to get the most out of a dance class. One of the most important things you can do is to attend every class. Reading a book, this one included, will not teach you how to dance or how to be an artist. You need the daily movement experience to make progress. A crash program in last-minute physical exercises before the final examination will only reward you with fatigue. If your school does not give a final movement examination, then you will probably be graded on your progress in your daily classroom work. If you are given a final movement examination, it will usually deal with the areas of movement that you have had in class and will be evaluated according to how well you understand and execute the movements. Whether you are given an exam or graded in the class, you can take out of the school only what you have gained as a person and as an artist. The pleasure of the experience and self-development should take precedence over grades, even if you are going on to graduate school.

Observing Movement

When the teacher demonstrates an exercise, watch carefully the flow of the movement and the exact positions the whole body and individual parts of the body take in space. Next, try to move through the exercise by physical suggestion of the positions rather than an all-out physical effort. This will develop your kinesthetic sense or motor memory—which are fancy words meaning simply the physical sensation you experience when you watch someone move, as in skating, dancing, falling, or jumping. Next try to do the movement as completely as possible. Watch the other dancers do the movement when you are not working and see if they are doing the same thing the teacher did. Watch the students who move well and ask yourself why they move well and apply it to your own movement. Watch the students who do not move as well and ask yourself why they are not as successful in the exercise. Observing the teacher, other students, and yourself trains your artistic eye to see the design of line, shapes, forms, and movement patterns—all elements of dance. Listen and apply immediately the criticisms your teacher gives you, as well as those given to the class in general. The criticism is offered to help you. It is not an attack on you personally, but rather a criticism to help you master technique. Your teacher is another pair of eyes working for you.

Developing a critical artistic eye is very important to the dancer, but a word of caution is in order. Asserting that you know more than the teacher or other students (even when you do) is undesirable in the classroom unless your opinions are asked for.

Having an open mind to any and all movement is extremely important to the dancer. This presupposes a cooperative spirit with the teacher and others in the classroom. A negative, noncooperative attitude will destroy the efforts of any teacher or fellow artist. A wise teacher—one who knows when to be firm and when to be light in approach—will encourage cooperation and a healthy climate of rapport. Good teachers recognize that intractable discipline and prodding are valid only when they benefit a potential talent. Your teacher will welcome intelligent questions and comments. You will gain the most from your classroom experience if you contribute to a spirit of cooperation and helpfulness.

MUSIC

In demonstrating an exercise, the teacher will usually count out 1 2 3, 1 2 3 4, 1 2 or some other combination of numbers. These individual numbers correspond to certain positions that the body or its parts assume in space or move through in space. When you are asked to repeat the movement, you should attempt to arrive at these positions on the counts the teacher has indicated. The counts are then repeated in the music that accompanies the dance sequence you are doing.

Other teachers, instead of giving you specific counts to reach a position on, will give you a phrase of movement that is to correspond to a like musical phrase. A phrase is a certain number of counts or positions that usually make a simple statement. The movement phrase could be likened to a sentence or fragment of a sentence within the spoken language.

A few teachers prefer not to use music, phrases, or counts. They attempt to get you to move so that you sense your own movements in a prescribed or not prescribed time. Whatever method or methods they use, you should know that dance is done in time as well as in space, and you should understand what happens when the same movements are done slowly or fast. Develop your musical sense so that you can move to the music or against the music when desired.

In most cases dance is performed to music or some other rhythmical accompaniment, so a basic understanding of common musical forms can be helpful to you. You will be expected to "keep time" with the music. If you study a musical instrument or take a beginning course in musical theory, it will help your dancing by developing your musical appreciation and knowledge. You can help develop your rhythmical sense, which will help you move in time to the beats, by listening to all kinds of music and tapping or clapping out the rhythmical pulse (beat) you feel. As an added exercise, you can try to analyze the structure of the musical piece. You might ask yourself such questions as how the composer has divided up the musical beats you feel, what kind of musical phrases he has used, what moods he has suggested, or what kind of transitions he has used to move from one mood to another mood. Later you might want to study specific musical forms such as the waltz, polka, or mazurka and try to identify these musical forms. If you like the modern sounds of the disco dances, you might enjoy trying to analyze the structure of these pieces. Try to decide why this music has such a universal appeal. Is it the insistent repetition of a basic beat or the subtle, shifting rhythms? Or is it the words?

There are some basic musical structures that all dancers work with, so you should have some understanding of them. When you watch someone unconsciously tapping his foot in time with a piece of music, he usually is tapping the floor *Beat* in unison with the heavy accents in the music. These are the strong beats that keep the dancers or musicians moving or playing in unison. There are also light beats that precede the repetitious heavy pulses in the music. A light beat occurs when the person you are watching lifts his toes from the floor. A heavy beat occurs when his toes strike the floor.

The light and heavy beats are usually divided into a specific number of counts that are repeated over and over. These repeating series of counts are called bars or measures. For example, two bars would be: 1 and 2 and 3 and 4 and; 1 and 2 and 3 and 4 and. Each of the bars in this example has four counts. The light beat is indicated by the "and," the heavy beat by the "count." Usually the first "count" of each bar is more heavily accented or sounded than the three following counts.

In the examples that follow we have listed the most common musical bars that you will probably encounter in your beginning work. (Notice that the "and" counts have been omitted.) The symbol > indicates the strong beat. The ⁄ indicates the secondary or lighter beat, which means that it is accented more heavily than the other counts but not as heavily as the first count of the bar. The two numbers written as a fraction constitute the musical time signature. The upper number shows how many counts there are in a bar, and the lower number shows what kind of a musical note gets one count. In 2/4 time, for example, there are two counts to a bar and a quarter note gets one. In learning dance, the upper number is more important. Try clapping the following rhythms, accenting the first count to get their rhythmical feeling.

Measure

Rhythm

$\frac{4}{4}$ $\overset{>}{1}$ 2 $\overset{\diagup}{3}$ 4, $\overset{>}{1}$ 2 $\overset{\diagup}{3}$ 4, $\overset{>}{1}$ 2 $\overset{\diagup}{3}$ 4

(three bars of four counts each)

$\frac{3}{4}$ $\overset{>}{1}$ 2 3, $\overset{>}{1}$ 2 3, $\overset{>}{1}$ 2 3

$\frac{2}{4}$ $\overset{>}{1}$ 2, $\overset{>}{1}$ 2, $\overset{>}{1}$ 2

$\frac{6}{8}$ $\overset{>}{1}$ 2 3 $\overset{\diagup}{4}$ 5 6, $\overset{>}{1}$ 2 3 $\overset{\diagup}{4}$ 5 6, $\overset{>}{1}$ 2 3 $\overset{\diagup}{4}$ 5 6

As you have noticed, the 6/8 rhythm has been stressed heavily on the first count and less heavily on the fourth count. Often a 6/8 rhythm is played very quickly by the musician, so is frequently more easily counted by the teacher as $\overset{>}{1}$ 2, $\overset{>}{1}$ 2.

The example shows how the counts would be written in musical notation.

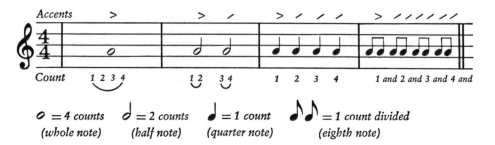

o = 4 counts
(whole note)

d = 2 counts
(half note)

$♩$ = 1 count
(quarter note)

$♪♪$ = 1 count divided
(eighth note)

A *triplet* occurs when three notes are played in the time alotted for one note.

The modern dance teacher often experiments with changes in the rhythmical form. The teacher may change the number of counts in the basic musical bars to give variety. You might be asked to dance to a series of bars like 1̄ 2 3, 1̄ 2 3 4, or 1̄ 2, 1̄ 2 3 or some other combination of rhythms. This is referred to as *mixed meter*.

Another musical change you might encounter in the dance class is called *shifted accent*. Instead of the first count, the accent falls on another count. For example:

1̄ 2 3, 1̄ 2 3, 1 2̄ 3, 1 2 3̄

1 2 3̄, 1 2̄ 3, 1̄ 2 3, 1̄ 2 3

In this example the expected heavy accent in the third, fourth, fifth, and sixth bars has been shifted to a count other than the first count, resulting in a feeling of syncopation. *Syncopation* can be shifting the accent, but is more often beginning a note on an unaccented beat and continuing the note without a new accent into the ordinarily accented beat. For example: clap the "ands" and "counts" of the following rhythm—*don't* clap the following count when it is tied together with a bow:

1̄ 2 3 and 1 2 3 and 1 2 3 and 1 2 3.

The silence on the count of one makes the syncopation.

Cumulative rhythm occurs when each new bar has one more count added to it. For example: 1̄, 1̄ 2, 1̄ 2 3, 1̄ 2 3 4.

Diminution of rhythm is the exact opposite of cumulative rhythm. Each new bar has one count subtracted from it. For example: 1̃ 2 3 4, 1̃ 2 3, 1̃ 2, 1̃.

Tempo refers to the speed of the musical accompaniment or dance movement. *Changes in tempo* from very slow to very fast or the reverse result in a change of the quality of the movement. If your teacher changes the tempo, observe the effect on the movement. Changes in tempo sometimes make otherwise dreary movement quite exciting to watch.

Dancers do not always dance with the reoccurring beat of the music. This would soon lead to boredom. To add interest the dancers also move on the "offbeat" or against the prevailing rhythm. If you clap the counts below with the accents indicated above them, you will feel the sense of *double time,* or doubling of the basic beat. Each of the bars should take exactly the same amount of time to clap.

1̃ 2̃ 3 4, 1̃ and 2 and 3 and 4 and, 1̃ 2̃ 3 4, 1̃ and 2 and 3 and 4 and

Part of the pleasure of the classroom experience will be the thrill of exploring with your teacher the various rhythmical possibilities, and also the qualities and forms of movement described in the next chapter. When the teacher has demonstrated and led you through a movement combination, your teacher will no doubt say something like "ready and one." The "ready" is your warning to ready yourself to move. The "and" tells you to set your body in motion to move into your first position on the count of "one."

Translating the rhythms and moods of the music into movements in space and time leads you toward the discipline that you must acquire if you are eventually to express to an audience your pleasure in moving. The same discipline will permit you to express your thoughts and feelings in dance. If you choose dance as a career, the discipline will help you contribute to your art as a dancer, choreographer, or teacher.

Technique Analysis

Chapter 3

What we do not understand,
we do not possess.
— Goethe

DEVELOPMENT
IN TECHNIQUE The development of modern dance as an art form came about by breaking the "rules" of what dance was "supposed" to be. The traditions and techniques of modern dance continue to evolve as new gifted artists change the rules. Such change is a healthy thing. An art form can grow only when new ideas and new modes of expression come into it.

One of the exciting elements of the modern dance is the distorted use of lines, shapes, and forms to achieve a new aesthetic of beauty. Any line, any shape, any form that the human body can possibly assume in space is valid to the modern dancer if it expresses what the dancer wants to communicate. Some of you in the beginning may think the movements you are asked to do are "ugly." If you should feel that way, think of the movements as a challenge to see if you can find any similar shapes and forms in the world around you, and then try to understand their validity in an art form.

Basic Alignment You should be aware of a few basic points about natural body alignment in order to understand the deviations from it. Think of your natural alignment as "good posture." Think of your body being lengthened upward from your foot support through the top of your head. The alignment is as if you were holding onto a bar over your head and hanging down from it. Think of a straight line running down from the top of your head through your neck, torso, pelvis, and legs. This line is the central axis of your body. When you are standing, jumping, kneeling, or sitting in a good posture, be aware that your head, chest, and pelvic area stay in a straight vertical line. Your shoulders should be comfortably directed sideward and downward.

People with bad posture may slump forward so that their shoulders are rounded, or release their pelvis backward, causing a sway-back. Avoid both distortions of line.

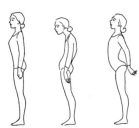

The following illustrations provide a few ideas for you to consider in your basic alignment.

You should hold good alignment through various degrees of *leg rotation*. The legs can be turned out from the hip socket or held so that the feet are pointed forward in a parallel position.

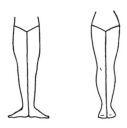

You should have *weight placement on the feet* evenly divided in a tripod between the big toe, the little toe, and the heel. When you rise to the ball of the foot (to half-toe), your weight should be between the big toe and the second toe, never toward the little toe.

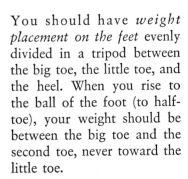

Good alignment of the leg is essential to support in a *knee bend*. You should keep the center of the knee in line with the middle toe. In the small knee bend (demi-plié), the heels usually remain on the floor. In the deep knee bend

(grand plié), the heels usually leave the floor naturally, in order to prevent a pushing backward in the pelvis with a subsequent lean forward in the torso. In the turned-out side position (second position) the heels usually remain on the floor.

To *balance on one leg,* you should lengthen upward on the vertical line through the body. Don't "sit" into the supporting leg. Shift the hip toward the supporting leg and on a slight diagonal upward. In the basic balance on one leg, keep the two front pelvic bones straight across on a horizontal line.

Terminology   In general, modern dancers have not codified the terms for positions and movements. A number of modern dancers feel that codification of terms would inhibit free expression and would prevent new forms of technique from developing. Another argument against codification is the infinite variety of positions the body can assume in space: any code of modern dance movement would have to be limited and arbitrary. We have attempted to give names to body positions *only as a guide* to analyzing the infinite movement possibilities of the body. The names should be thought of as a springboard to further exploration and body analysis and not as an attempt at definitive codification.

Terms vary from one teacher to another. Learn the terms your own teacher uses so that upon hearing instructions you will be able to respond with the desired movement. For the purposes of analysis, definitions of basic positions are desirable. Then you as a student can identify each basic position and can understand the further development of that position. This helps you learn faster and helps to train the "artistic eye" to see the subtleties of movement.

FIRST ANALYSIS   Movements in a Stationary Position

While in a stationary position, you have only a few basic possibilities of movement: you may bend (tilt), rotate, shift, or support yourself in various ways. Despite the limited number of basic movements, many variations are possible, and a stationary position presents opportunities as well as restrictions. The drawings on the next page show a few of the variations.

The *whole leg* can bend from the hip socket and move in any direction, to a certain level, with or without rotation in the hip socket and with or without a bend in the lower leg. The first illustration indicates various levels of the arm and leg in the side direction. The leg is limited in the degree of level it can achieve, but flexibility in the shoulder socket allows the arm to make a full circle (360°) passing through the various levels in the side direction, as well as forward or back.

Bend (tilt)

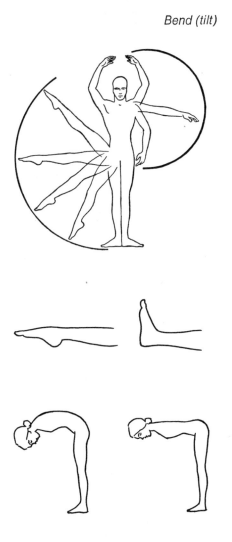

The *foot* can stretch forward to a "pointed" foot position or bend back to a "flexed" foot position, with or without rotation. The *arm* and *hand* have more freedom of movement, but are similar to the leg and foot in bending with or without rotation. The *torso* can bend in any direction with a rounded back or straight back, to a specific level, with or without body rotation. The bend or tilt can be in the chest or pelvic area (more limited bending) or from the hip joints (greater bending). The *head-neck* can bend in some direction that is independent from the position of the torso.

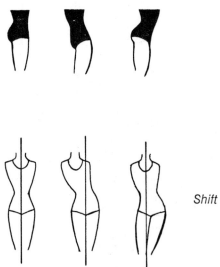

Rotate The *torso* and its individual parts can all rotate around their own axes separately or together. The individual parts of the torso—*head, rib cage,* and *pelvis*—can do a kind of rotary action forward, backward, and sideward. The motion is more of a rocking action as opposed to the bend or tilt of those parts. The whole body can revolve completely around on its own axis (turn).

Shift The *head, shoulders, rib cage,* and *pelvis* can shift as a unit from their central axis in some direction.

Support The *body* can be supported on the floor by sitting, kneeling, lying, or standing. It can leave the support by jumping or being lifted and held.

As a means of movement and position analysis you could ask yourself various questions. Concerning bending, you could inquire: What part of the body is bending and to what level? Is the bend curved or sharply angled?

About rotation you could ask: What part or parts are rotated and in what direction? If the whole body is turning, is it a complete turn or only a fraction of a turn? Is the turn on one foot or both feet? What is the position of the body in the turn?

As for shifting, you could raise two questions: What part of the body is being displaced, and in what direction? Is the shift only a basic impulse to move into another position?

And about support (or nonsupport) of the body you could ask: Is a new body support achieved by jumping or rising upward to the balls of the feet? Or is it arrived at by sinking downward to small or large knee bends or positions of kneeling, sitting, or lying? What positions are moved through to arrive at the new support?

Dance is, of course, more than just stationary positions. Dance involves moving the whole body through space from one position to another. The motivation behind the movement will change the look and feel of the movement.

SECOND ANALYSIS   Body Lines

Three basic lines can be achieved in dance. These lines may be formed by parts of the body or by the dancer's entire body as shown in the illustrations:

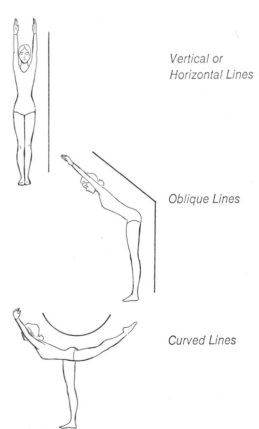

Vertical or horizontal lines occur when the dancer stands upright or bends at a right angle or lies on the floor. Such lines also may be achieved in many other ways.

Vertical or Horizontal Lines

Oblique (slanted) lines occur when the dancer bends at an obtuse or an acute angle in relation to either a horizontal or a vertical. Oblique lines may be formed in many ways.

Oblique Lines

Curved lines occur in various positions. These lines may be combined with the others, just as oblique lines may be combined with horizontals or verticals or both.

Curved Lines

26   As line is so important in the dance, you should *visually* trace the line of movement your teacher demonstrates and try to approximate it. Sometimes you may think another line looks better or feels better for you, but remember that part of the self-discipline of learning the dance craft is to make your body do anything that choreography requires.

THIRD ANALYSIS   *Feet, Body, and Arm Positions*

Feet Positions   Many modern dancers use some version of the following feet positions with the legs either parallel or turned outward or inward from the hip sockets. The first illustrations indicate the usual degree of turnout for the beginning level.

First   In the *first* position, the heels are together (closed).

Second   In the *second* position, the heels are about twelve inches apart (open side).

Third   The front heel is next to the instep of the back foot and the feet are touching in the *third* position (closed heel to instep).

Fourth   In the *fourth* position, one foot is about twelve inches in front of the other. The heels may be in line (not crossed over) or the heel of the front foot may be in line with the toes of the back foot (crossed over—open forward-backward).

Fifth   The front heel is next to the toe of the back foot and the feet are touching in the *fifth* position (closed toe-to-heel).

Here are four modifications of the first position:

The *full turnout* modification requires turn-out in the hip sockets so that the toes point directly to the sides of the body.

Full Turnout

In the *parallel* version, the legs are not turned out or in, and the toes point forward. The feet may be touching or slightly separated. Some teachers prefer that the legs be slightly separated so that the hip sockets and the bones of the legs are in a more natural alignment.

Parallel

In the *diagonal-in* modification, the legs are turned in from the hip sockets so that the toes point on diagonal lines inward (this position is occasionally used in modern dance).

For purposes of analysis, the following definitions hold. The definitions use the basic foot positions as reference points. As the illustrations show, the definitions include various body lines as well as movements in a stationary position.

Body Positions

In the *first* position, the feet and legs are together.

Standing   Sitting   Bending

In the *second* position, the feet and legs are apart to the side.

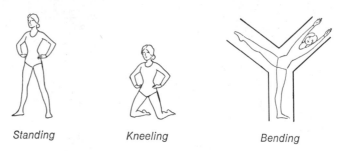

Standing   Kneeling   Bending

In the *fourth* position, the feet and legs are apart, one foot to the front and the other to the back.

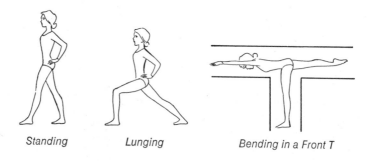

Standing   Lunging   Bending in a Front T

In the *third* or *fifth* position, the legs and feet cross one another in some manner (the third and the fifth positions are combined here because the placement of feet is so similar).

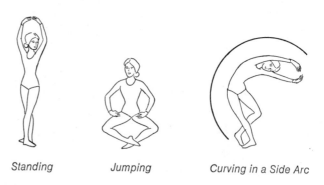

Standing   Jumping   Curving in a Side Arc

Arm Positions   Because the arm is more flexible than other parts of the body, more movement possibilities exist. Not all schools will agree with the analysis below. Other basic arm positions may be defined. The descriptions and illustrations are presented here only as a guide to analysis. The first illustrations show curved arms.

In the *first* position, the arms are down at the sides of the body (down).

In the *second* position, the arms are raised to the sides of the body in a horizontal plane (side).

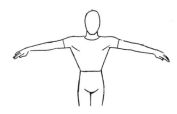

One arm is raised to the side and the other arm is to the front—high or middle or low —in the *third* position (front-side).

The arms are in front of the body but not on the same level in the *fourth* position (front —different levels).

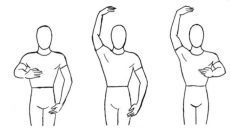

In the *fifth* position, the arms are in front of the body and are on the same level (front— same levels).

Examples of some variations of these arm positions follow. (With bending in the torso or rotations in the shoulder sockets, the positions also can be approximated behind the back.) The illustrations show angular arm positions. Here the upper arm determines the basic direction.

First   Second   Third

Fourth   Fifth

You might want to experiment, using the basic positions as a guide, to see how many variations you can discover by rotating the arms in the sockets, by changing the directions and levels of the arms, and by changing the degree of bend in the elbows.

In watching classroom demonstrations, ask the same sorts of questions that were applied to the analysis of movements in a stationary position: Are the arms straight or bent? In what direction? What is the angle of bend? Are the arms rotated inward or outward? Is the basic line curved or angular?

FOURTH ANALYSIS   *Movement*

Dance is, of course, more than static positions in space. Some schools simplify the analysis of movement into two categories: *nonlocomotor movement,* which means movement around your own axis, above a stationary support, and *locomotor movement,* which means movement through space to get yourself from one place to another.

In our analysis of basic movements in a stationary position—bending, rotating, shifting, and going to various support positions—we described nonlocomotor movements. However, these movements also can be done while moving from one place to another. Similarly, many of the movements described below can be done *either* while traveling in space or while remaining in one place.

Various kinds of movement analyses follow. If you imagine these kinds of movements combined together into a movement sequence, you can begin to appreciate the interrelationship of your body and the space through which it moves. How the movement is done (quality or dynamics) and why the movement is done (motivation) provide infinite variations.

Your body can descend toward the floor, as in a deep knee bend, or rise away from the floor, as in a jump. The individual parts of your body also can move toward or away from the floor. Falls and recovery are another common form of descending and rising. There are two basic kinds of falls. In one you momentarily fall off balance and then quickly re-establish your equilibrium or control. Body swings from side to side are an example. In the second you go with the natural momentum of the action until it has come to rest or until it rebounds (recovers) in another direction. For example, you fall to the floor and then rise up again. Both movements are controlled partly by gravity and partly by the will of the dancer. Falls, or dropping and recovering, can be done with the whole body or with only a part of it.

Descending or Rising Movement

The various parts of the body can move up-down, forward-backward, sideward away from or across the body, or in diagonals between front-side and back-side. And of course the whole body also can move front-back, side left or right, up-down, or on the diagonal.

Directions of Movement

An outward movement is any kind of movement that goes away from your body, as in a leg kick to the front. An inward movement is any kind of movement that comes toward the center of your body, as when you pull your outstretched arms toward your chest.

Gestures of the arms and legs can take place away from your body so that the emphasis may be spatially oriented. When the gestures of arms and legs take place near your body, the emphasis may be more body oriented.

Far and Near Movement

32   *Curved and*
Straight Paths

The whole body or a part of the body can move through space in a curved line, that is, an arclike movement. For example, if you swing your arm in a large circle, the finger tips are tracing a circular path in space. The illustration indicates another curve pattern.

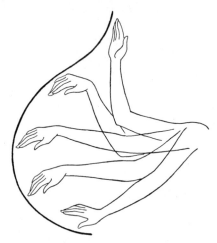

Movements can emphasize a straight line in space (spoke-like) by moving toward or away from the body, or by tracing a line from one point in space to another, as shown in the illustration.

Turns

There are four kinds of turns: (1) You can twist or rotate *part of your body* on its central axis. (2) You can turn *your whole body* around in a circle. There are many ways such turns can be done; for example, on your own axis on two feet, on one foot, from one foot to the other foot, or while jumping. (3) You can turn in a *traveling pattern*; for example, by walking in a circle around a chair or by doing a series of turns while traveling in a straight line. (4) The whole body (or certain parts of it) can turn, as in a somersault or cartwheel revolution, or as in nodding or shaking the head. In the examples given above, (1) and (2) are non-locomotor movement, but (3) is locomotor. Number 4 may be either, depending upon whether the whole body is used.

Movement of the entire body in some direction through space is called *traveling*. There are many ways of traveling and they employ the other movement patterns. The following movements could be done in place as well as traveling: (1) *walk*, (2) *run*, (3) *jump*. Jumps can be analyzed in terms of whether the jump starts from one foot or two feet and lands on one foot or two feet. There are five possibilities: from both feet to both feet, from one foot to the other foot, from one foot to the same foot, from one foot to the two feet, and from both feet to one foot. The Labanotation system of analysis defines those movements respectively as jump, leap, hop, assemblé, and sissonne.

TRAVELING (Locomotor Movements)

Whether or not these specific terms are used, recognizing the kind of preparation and landing for a jump can help you see and learn movement sequences more quickly. If you recognize, for example, that a jump starts from two feet and lands on two feet, you can quickly begin to look for other details like the rotation of the legs, whether the legs are straight or bent, whether the feet are pointed or flexed, and so forth.

The visual results of the walk, run, and jump will be changed by whether or not the use of the legs is stressed or unstressed, whether or not there is greater or lesser use of energy to travel upward or outward through space, and the direction in which the movement travels.

Movements sometimes used in modern dance follow. Some can be done either in place or traveling. (1) *Skip* by doing a step and a hop alternating from one foot to the other with uneven rhythm. The skip might also start with the hop followed by the step. (2) *Step-hop* by stepping on one foot and hopping on the same foot. The rhythm may be even or uneven. (3) The terms *gallop* or *slip step* and *slide* are open to individual interpretation. Follow the interpretation of your teacher if these actions are used in the

Variations

classroom. For purposes of analysis only, slide by sliding the front foot forward, transferring the weight to the front foot; then slide the back foot toward the front foot, placing the weight onto the back foot with a "cutting action" that forces the front foot to lift quickly, but with very little rise and fall of the body. The gallop or slip step is similar to the slide except that there is a jump into the air as the weight is transferred from one foot to the other. Children demonstrate similar action when riding an imaginary galloping horse. (4) *Prance* like a trotting horse by stepping alternately on each foot and lifting the free leg with the knee bent. (5) A *triplet* is made up of three steps on alternating feet. The knee is bent slightly on the first step, but the legs are straight on the next two steps, and the steps are on the balls of the feet. The body moves *down, up, up, down, up, up* as the knee is bent alternately on one leg and then the other. In music a triplet is three notes that equal one quarter note. Some teachers teach the dance triplet the same way. Others treat the triplet as three steps done to three beats in the music, in other words, a waltz. (6) *Swings* can be done with individual parts of the body or with the whole body. Swings have the quality or action of the pendulum on a clock as it traces an arclike path between two points—rising, falling, rising. The rising action is increasingly sustained and the falling action is increasingly quickened.

Body and Spatial Design   The body, either at rest or moving, creates a form or shape in space. The body as a whole creates one kind of shape and the spaces around the body create another kind. These shapes may be seen as straight or curved lines and are altered by the changing relationships of the body parts to one another. In symmetrical design the body parts are equally proportioned in the space, and in asymmetrical design the body parts are not equally proportioned. The two illustrations indicate symmetry-asymmetry and the primary-secondary design of the body and the space around it.

A second kind of space can be seen by movement in opposite directions, that is, either forward-backward, sideward out-sideward across, or up-down. The direction of the movement changes the general movement shape, which can be perceived respectively as advancing-retreating, widening-narrowing, or rising-sinking. The illustration suggests the movement shape of advancing-retreating.

A third kind of spatial or body design is the adaptation of the body to objects or to another person. In dance this kind of adaptation, or sculpting of space, is often done without an actual object present. The illustration shows body adaptation in partner work.

FIFTH ANALYSIS   *Qualities or Dynamics*

All movement patterns take on a different look when you change their qualities or dynamics. If a pattern fails to convey some quality, it becomes devoid of any human association, and it will have little appeal to a general audience.

Qualities are related to the science of *dynamics*. Dynamics, which concerns the motion of bodies and their motivating forces, is related to the greater or lesser use of energy by your body while moving in time and space. The movement may be motivated by the need to express some kind of emotional or physical state. There are a number of basic qualities that can add "shading" to your movement in the same way a painter uses contrasts in colors and shapes to enrich a painting.

The inner motivation for the movement is elusive, but the external movement can be analyzed. For purposes of analysis only, we have divided the qualities or dynamics into the four efforts conceptualized by Rudolf Laban and F. C. Lawrence (*see* Bibliography). The four efforts are time, flow, weight, and space. For each, the degree of effort used can be any point between two extremes. It is the mover's attitude toward a particular effort that determines how that person moves. In life the kind of movement quality or effort used is in a state of flux adapting to internal or external needs of the moment. In dance the dancer can consciously concentrate on changing the effort quality or qualities to add texture or shading to the movement, thereby enriching a sequence of movements.

Time   Movement may be sustained or sudden. Sustained movement can be thought of as leisurely, indulging in the use of time. Sudden movement or a series of quick motions conveys a sense of urgency.

Flow   Movement tension may be free or bound. Free flow can be thought of as unrestricted, not holding back. Bound flow can be thought of as restricted, held back. (No negative connotation is intended by the term bound.)

Weight   Weight may be light or strong. Light weight can be thought of as delicate and rarified, overcoming the pull of gravity. Strong weight can be thought of as forcefully increasing the pressure or push as the body follows the pull of gravity. (Strong weight is not synonymous with the heaviness of a person or an object.)

Space   Spatial attention may be indirect or direct. Indirect spatial attention is characterized as flexible, with many overlapping foci or many shifts of attention. Direct spatial attention is focused or channeled into a single spatial focus. Again, it is an inner attitude toward the space so that eye contact or movement of the body may not necessarily reinforce indirect or direct attention.

Some movement experiments may help you sense these efforts. Suppose you were given the following movement assignments. How would you move? Do these assignments influence your attitude toward the effort quality in some way?

Time: (Sustained) Lie down on the floor and stand up as slowly as you can. (Sudden) Lie down and stand up as quickly as you can. *Flow:* (Free) With as little tension as possible, move about the room freely swinging your upper body and arms. (Bound) Start to increase the tension or restrict the freedom of the movement until it feels as if you are fighting to hold back the movement. *Weight:* (Light) Starting curled up on the floor, unfold your body as if it were a balloon being filled with helium; let the action float you up to a standing position. (Strong) Reverse the previous action, from standing to curling. Really get behind your weight and strongly push it downward as you lower yourself to the floor. *Space:* (Indirect) Move to different places in the room, rapidly changing your focus and direction. (Direct) Focus all your attention on one place in the room and move to it directly.

All teachers are unique and have their own terms to help you understand dynamic forces and how the same movement changes when the quality is changed. Some teachers use word imagery or a descriptive phrase that suggests the quality. For example: *sustained,* prolonging the movement; *vibratory,* shaking or trembling; *percussive,* beating or striking; *suspension,* a moment when the movement is lifted and held, and so forth. Try to sense in your body the quality described and how it can alter the movement.

A dance movement phrase usually has a unity or logical coherence that creates a sense of harmony or completeness, which in turn leads into the next phrase. One could think of it as a movement statement with a beginning, development, and transition that leads into the next statement. The next statement might be a development of the original phrase or an independent new movement statement. When music (or sound) accompanies the movement, the dance phrase may or may not accompany the musical phrase. Learning to recognize and recreate the ebb and flow of your teacher's or your own movements will bring you nearer to the goal of being able to express yourself through movement. Following are some general ideas that might aid in analyzing

Emphasis in a Movement Phrase

what the movement phrases are about and where they are going: (1) How does the sequence start, that is, what is the first movement? (2) What is the tempo or rate of speed? (3) Does the movement have a sense of freedom or of being held back? (4) Is there a sense of lightness, free of gravity, or does the movement suggest getting behind your weight and directing it somewhere? (5) Does the movement appear spatially focused or diffused? (6) Are the movements confined or limited to use of the space around your body, or do they use a great deal of space around the room? (7) Does the sequence of movement flow harmoniously, or is it disjointed? (8) Is the shape of the body usually symmetrical (balanced proportion of design) or asymmetrical (unbalanced proportion of design)? (9) Do the gestures and movement tend to be curved (arclike) or linear (spokelike)? (10) Is a movement accented with more force in a direction upward, downward, inward, or outward? (11) Does any movement seem to be an impulse (impelling force) leading into another movement? (12) Is there any repetitive or stressed directional movement pattern, floor pattern, or rhythmic pattern? (13) What seem to be the distinctive elements that are emphasized in the movement—rhythm, body form, line, floor pattern, or something else? (14) Can you verbalize, rhythmically, descriptive words that match the movement sequence, for example, fast-fast-slow, up-down-out, sharp-smooth-sharp, push-pull-slash, step-step-hop, and so forth? (15) Is a characteristic manner or expression important to the movement? (16) Is there a motive or a central theme that unifies the movement?

Whether or not one follows or uses these kinds of dynamic analyses is not important. Modern dance grows by the diversity of approaches. What is important is developing your ability to see others' use of dynamics, and to sense your own. This ability can help you learn a movement phrase, how it starts, how it develops, how it concludes, how it makes the transition to the next phrase. By learning movement sequences dynamically, you can escape the possibility of learning a series of disconnected steps and postures without the inherent motivating and unifying spirit. Also important in modern dance, an appreciation of dynamics allows you to begin to understand and find your own way of moving and how movement can be used for self-expression through dance.

Basically, floor patterns are made up of curves, straight lines, or combinations of both. Patterns may be more intricate than the paths of movement described above. A few of the basic patterns are shown below. As a means of movement exploration, try applying these basic floor patterns to movement patterns or to stationary positions of the body. (They all can be done with the whole body or parts of the body.) The arrow indicates the direction of travel and the square represents the performance area.

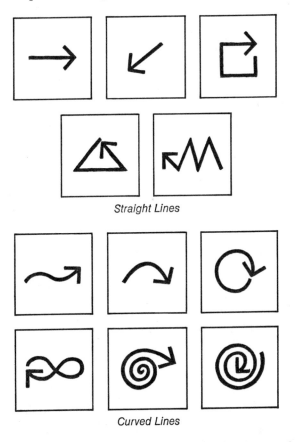

Straight Lines

Curved Lines

These six sets of analyses are offered to help you learn to dance more quickly by using your mind as well as your body. Your teacher will stress some of these ideas and reject others. All approaches are valid if they help you reach your goal as a dancer.

Anatomy, Injuries, Diet

Chapter 4

*Frequently the most talented people are those
most aware of their own deficiencies and most willing
to work hard to overcome them.*
— Lee Strasberg

BASIC ANATOMY   It is to your advantage to be familiar with the terms your teacher uses when referring to anatomy. There are definite correct and incorrect ways to work your body to receive the maximum results from your effort. If you know what part of the body your teacher is talking about, you can immediately apply your anatomical knowledge to the correct execution of the exercise.

We are presenting to you only the basic anatomical facts and physiological principles from which to work. If you are interested in a more thorough study, we have listed some excellent references in the selected readings.

In a single dance exercise almost every muscle in the body is used. In the charts that follow we have indicated only the large, main groups of movers and their common functions and movements. You can dance without knowing about these muscles, but a brief introduction to them should help you to understand dance movement better.

INJURIES, ETC.   A vigorous dance class after a period of inactivity may cause
Muscle Soreness   muscle soreness, the most common pain resulting from dance classes. Although it is uncomfortable, the pain is temporary and is not debilitating. At the moment when you are sore you may feel as if you could not take another step, let alone take a dance class. There are many theories why the muscles become so sore. Regardless of the reason, the best way to relieve your pain is to work the muscle again,

and as soon as possible. A hot bath or shower and a massage feel marvelous, but actually do little more than relax you and make you feel better temporarily.

Pain from Injuries

Pain resulting from an injury is an entirely different feeling, and proper care of the injured part must be administered to prevent possible permanent damage. For the most part, an injury occurs when a part of your body is weak and/or when you are tired physically or psychologically or both. In any class, if you are in good physical condition and if you work correctly, injuries should rarely occur. However, a few common physical problems are discussed here. It is assumed that if you have severe, recurring pain, you will see your doctor, and if you have any injury, you will report it to your teacher.

Cramp

A common pain is the cramp. A cramp is an overfatigue of a muscle and is probably caused from a lack of calcium and salt in the diet. It usually occurs in the arch of the foot or the calf of the leg. The pain occurs because the muscle goes into a maximum contraction involuntarily. To relieve a cramp, try to stretch the cramped part very gently or massage it in order to get a fresh blood supply to it. Generally, no permanent damage results from a cramp, but the muscle may be sore. Usually you may continue dancing as soon as severe pain subsides.

Sprain

A much more serious injury is the sprain. This injury occurs to a joint when a bone goes past its normal range of movement and tissue is torn. This does not heal easily and demands a doctor's care. Ligaments and capsules in the hip and shoulder may be injured in this manner, but more commonly the injury takes place in the ligaments of the ankle. Generally, something wet and cold should be applied to the area until a doctor can be consulted. He should be called or the injured dancer taken to him immediately. To prevent a sprained ankle it is extremely important that the ankle be centered with the knee at all times, especially when landing from a jump or leap. To prevent a sprain in the hip, you must never turn out beyond your range. If you are prone to a sprain in any part of your body, consult your doctor or teacher for exercises to strengthen that part.

Strain

A strain is caused when a muscle is overtired from constant irritation by overcontraction of muscles. It affects muscle tendons and soft tissue. This pain can be relieved by rest. It usually happens in the gastrox (calf muscle) and

PART OF BODY	MAIN MUSCLES	APPROXIMATE LOCATION	MAIN MOVEMENT
ARMS AND SHOULDER	TRICEPS	Bottom of upper arm (when arm is lifted to side at right angle to body with palm up)	Straightens or extends elbow
	BICEPS	Top of upper arm (when arm is lifted to side at right angle to body with palm up)	Bends or flexes elbow
	PECTORALS	Front of chest	Rotate arm inward in shoulder socket and control some other arm movements
	TRAPEZIUS AND OTHER MUSCLES OF THE UPPER BACK	Upper back	Move scapulae (shoulder blades)
ABDOMEN	OBLIQUES	Over ribs on either side	Twists upper body to either side
	RECTUS ABDOMINIS	From upper ribs to top of pubic bone, covering abdomen area	Raises upper body forward as in sit-up
	QUADRATUS LUMBORUM	Small of back	1. Bends upper body to side 2. Stabilizes pelvis and spine
HIP AND UPPER LEG (THIGH)	GLUTEALS	Buttocks	1. Stabilize hip 2. Extend hip
	QUADRICEPS	Front of thigh	Extends leg in forward movements
	HAMSTRINGS	Back of upper leg	Bend knee
LOWER LEG	GASTROCNEMIUS (GASTROX OR CALF)	Back of lower leg	1. Points foot 2. *Raises* leg to ball of foot (half toe) 3. Bends knee
	SOLEUS	Back of lower leg under gastrox muscle	*Holds* leg in half-toe position (ball of foot)
	TIBIALIS AND PERONEUS	Around either side of ankle	Move ankle in circle
	ACHILLES TENDON	Lower part of leg and heel on back of leg; lower part of gastrox (calf) muscle	Same as gastrox

COMMON EXERCISE TO STRENGTHEN OR USE	SIGNIFICANCE TO DANCE	COMMON INJURY AND PREVENTION
Push up	1. Strengthens arms for falls and lifts 2. Gives firmness under the arm	None
Push up and pull up	Strengthens arms for falls and lifts	None
Push up	1. Provides firm chest muscles 2. Needed for lifts and falls	None
Push up	Gives control of back and arms	None
Twist or rotate upper body	Makes small, strong waist	None
Sit up	Keeps abdomen flat if used constantly	None
1. Bend upper body to side 2. Sit up	Contributes to strong lower back	*Injury*—General weakness *Prevention*—Use.
1. Turn out the leg from hip socket 2. Lift leg to back	Contributes to thigh turn-out	None
1. Lift leg forward 2. Straighten leg at knee joint 3. Pull up knee cap	1. Steadies knee joint 2. Straightens knee 3. Provides stability for knee joint	*Injury*—Charley-horse *Prevention*—At onset of pain, rest until pain stops
1. Touch toes with fingers without bending knees 2. Sit erect on floor with legs extended straight forward 3. Bend knees	1. Bend knee 2. Must be stretched constantly	*Injury*—Cramps *Prevention*—At onset of pain, rest until pain stops
1. Jump 2. *Rise* to ball of foot	1. Tires easily 2. Main muscle in jump	*Injury*—Temporary soreness from sudden overuse *Prevention*—Should be used constantly
Rise to ball of foot and *hold*	1. Points foot 2. *Holds* leg in half-toe position	None
Rotate ankle in circle	1. Help protect Achilles tendon 2. Support ankle in all foot movements	*Injury*—Sprained ankle *Prevention*—Keep ankle in line with center of knee
Jump	1. Must be stretched constantly 2. Thickest and strongest tendon in body	*Injury*—Tears apart by violent overstretching *Prevention*—When coming down from a jump, land on ball of foot, lower heel to floor, bend leg

Charley-Horse

Shin Splint

Proper Rest

DIET

hamstrings (back of thigh). Strains rarely result from taking just one class.

The charley-horse is an injury which usually occurs in the quadriceps (front of thigh) and can be remedied by standing on the leg and massaging it gently.

A more serious injury is the shin splint. This occurs only to the muscles on the front of the tibia (shin bone). Shin splints are believed to be the tearing of the muscle from the bone, which may cause severe pain. An improper landing from a jump with the heels off the floor and with no bend in the knee seems to cause shin splints. A doctor should always be consulted when shin splints or any other injury occurs.

Other kinds of injuries could occur in a dance class, but they are few and very uncommon. It cannot be stressed enough that if you work properly, injuries should not occur.

Proper rest is one of the most important ways to prevent injuries. Many times injuries occur because the dancer is exhausted physically, psychologically, or both. You will probably be working or going to school full-time, in addition to studying dance. With this double burden, you must establish your priorities so that you are able to rest and get enough sleep for your needs.

Modern dance should not produce the bulky muscles familiar to a football player or a wrestler. These sport activities warrant the development of heavy muscles for strength. As a dancer you need long, lean lines so that the clarity of the movement is not clouded. You need minimum weight so that you can perform intricate movements easily.

You as a dancer must convey the ideal physique or figure. No one has a perfect body! But by proper dance training and a proper balance of exercise, rest, and diet, you can more quickly achieve the illusion of the ideal.

Dancers are notoriously abusive of their bodies. They often expect their bodies to respond instantly and perfectly on command without having given them proper care. You cannot expect to deal with the great physical demands made on your body without intelligently caring for it.

The word "diet" often suggests hunger, regimented eating, or eating only certain kinds of food for extended periods. To the dancer, diet should signify temperance in living habits.

As a dancer, you cannot afford extra calories in foods which do not make an appreciable contribution to your body. Even if you are of a good weight, size, and structure to be a dancer, it is to your advantage to evaluate your daily intake of food.

Your body needs specific foods every day. You need at least two portions of a high-protein food such as meat, poultry, fish, eggs, peas, or beans. You need one or more servings of green or yellow vegetables, and one or more servings of fruit (including citrus fruits). In addition, you should have two servings of a cereal product (this includes bread). You should have milk or milk products daily.

Specific Needs

You need a normal amount of salt and other vitamins and minerals daily. Salt should not be eliminated from the dancer's diet as the dancer sweats a great deal and loss of salt through perspiration can cause extreme exhaustion and even prostration during class. (It also is extremely important that a dancer drink from four to six glasses of water a day to offset loss of water through perspiration.) You should continue your normal intake of salt and not worry about it except during excessive heat or prolonged exercise.

Certain fad diets seem to be the folly of the dancer. Because you are dancing and must keep your strength level high, be sure that you do not eliminate proteins, vegetables, fruits, milk products, and whole grain cereals from your diet. It is important and relatively easy to eliminate fried foods, pastries, and carbonated beverages containing sugar.

The following is a suggested way to evaluate your eating habits. First, keep an *exact* record of the amount of everything you eat for three days. Do not change the way you usually eat. Buy a small calorie counter and count the number of calories you have consumed in these three days. Divide by three and you will find the average amount you eat daily. To lose one pound a week permanently, you have to cut 500 calories a day from your diet, provided you have not increased your activity level. If you increase the amount you exercise, you can lose weight at a faster rate. Often, though, exercise increases your appetite and weight is gained, not lost. Exercise may tone your muscles and you may find your measurements are smaller, but you have not lost weight. You must find a point of balance between exercise and food intake. As a rough guide, 3,500 calories make up one pound of fat.

Evaluating Your Diet

A female dancer can usually determine the amount of calories her body needs to *maintain* the desired weight by multiplying her weight by eleven or twelve, depending upon her metabolic rate (the rate she burns up food). This means if her desired weight is 100 pounds, she can probably maintain it by eating 1,100 to 1,200 calories a day. A male should be able to multiply his weight by twelve or thirteen or perhaps more to maintain his desired weight. Your individual needs will depend on how much you exercise and whether or not you have reached maturity. Of course, it is assumed that you will *consult your doctor before starting any diet* to make sure your overweight or underweight condition is not due to an illness.

A dancer, it seems, cannot be too slim. It is important, though, that with the extreme slimness of the dancer there is also a high degree of physical strength. If you are slim but weak, we suggest you see your doctor for a check-up. As far as dance is concerned, slimness on the female body is an asset, as long as this slimness is not an indication of poor health. The male dancer's physique should be well-muscled without excess fat or bulk.

Here, in brief, are some important guides to dieting: (1) Try not to eat between meals. If you must eat, try raw carrots, celery, turnips, radishes, or cauliflower. Drink water. (2) Eat at least three normal meals a day or five smaller meals. (Make sure they are small.) (3) Eat fresh fruit and low-calorie gelatine, sherbet, or custard for dessert. (4) If you must splurge on a high-calorie food item, then you must make up for it the next day by lowering the calorie intake. (5) Coffee and tea have zero calories provided they have no sugar and cream added to them. (6) Drink four to six glasses of water a day. You will be burning fat and a large intake of water helps elimination.

History

Chapter 5

For last year's words belong to last year's language
And next year's words await another voice.
— T. S. Eliot

The dance discussed in this book has been developed in the last eighty years. It was called "modern" because it broke from the traditions and the disciplines of the stiff formality of the ballet of the last century. At the beginning, modern dance was a way of life, an expression of the freedom of spirit, unfettered by outdated traditions and wornout beliefs. Modern dance was in its adolescence at the time of the movement for women's suffrage, Prohibition, World War I, and new movements in art. One such movement was called expressionism. Expressionism, which originated in painting, is a subjective expression of the artist's personal reaction to events or objects through distortion, abstraction, or symbols. It was a dominating influence on the modern dance.

PIONEERS IN DANCE

Many artists late in the last century were in search of a means to express their individuality and concern for man. Modern dance was one of the ways some of these people sought to free their creative spirit. At the beginning there was no exacting technique, no foundation from which to build. In later years trial, error, and genius founded the techniques and the principles of the movement. Eventually, innovators even drew from what they considered the dread ballet, but first they had to discard all that was academic so that the new could be discovered. The beginnings of modern dance were happening before Isadora Duncan, but she was the first person to bring the new dance to general audiences and see it accepted and acclaimed.

Isadora Duncan, 1878–1927

47

Her search for a natural movement form sent her to nature. She believed movement should be as natural as the swaying of the trees and the rolling waves of the sea, and should be in harmony with the movements of the earth. These beautiful ideals have often been misinterpreted and grossly misused in dance. Modern dance has often been thought of as young girls imitating the blooming of a flower. Contrary to popular belief, Miss Duncan never improvised on stage and personally supervised every detail of her performances. Her great contributions are in three areas.

First, she began the expansion of the kinds of movements that could be used in dance. Before Miss Duncan danced, ballet was the only type of dance performed in concert. In the ballet the feet and legs were emphasized, with virtuosity shown by complicated, codified positions and movements. Isadora performed dance by using all her body in the freest possible way, taking her inspiration from the ancient Greeks. She did not develop a technique as we know it today. Her dance stemmed from her soul and spirit. She was one of the pioneers who broke tradition so others might be able to develop the art.

Her second contribution lies in dance costume. She discarded corset, ballet shoes, and stiff costumes. These were replaced with flowing Grecian tunics, bare feet, and unbound hair. She believed in the natural body being allowed to move freely, and her dress displayed this ideal.

Her third contribution was in the use of music. In her performances she used the symphonies of great masters, including Beethoven and Wagner, which was not the usual custom.

She was as exciting and eccentric in her personal life as in her dance. Her two beautiful, illegitimate children who were tragically drowned, her many loves, and her death by strangulation from a long trailing scarf that accidentally wrapped around the wheel of a sports car—all these symbolize her dramatic life. She threw away the conventions which characterized the time in which she lived, 1878-1927. She has been portrayed in the film, *The Loves of Isadora,* and the dancing in this film is a near duplication of the way Miss Duncan moved.

Ruth St. Denis, 1877–1968

While Isadora Duncan had looked to the West and classical Greece for inspiration in her new dance, Ruth St. Denis had looked to the East and the Orient to discover a new movement form. In 1906 she performed *Radha,* a dance which used an Oriental theme to communicate a spiritual message. It was so significant that it continued to be performed even in the 1940s when Miss Ruth was in her sixties. She was interested not just in virtuosity in dance but in communicating an idea. She did not develop a technique. Instead she believed music was to be "visualized" in order to produce dance movements.

In the scheme of the development of modern dance, Ruth St. Denis holds a vital position. She not only made specific contributions of her own but also provided, through the Denishawn Company, a proving ground for the next generation of dancers, including Martha Graham, Doris Humphrey, and Charles Weidman. Denishawn, which was a partnership and a marriage between Miss Ruth and Ted Shawn, proved successful for some sixteen years. During these years Denishawn was financially self-supporting, a unique position in the history of modern dance companies.

Ted Shawn was co-director of Denishawn, and if Miss Ruth was its spirit, he was its form. He performed and choreographed in Denishawn until it dissolved. In the early 1930s he formed a company of male dancers who were ex-athletes. He was influenced by François Delsarte who in the early nineteenth century developed a technique of pantomime that honestly expressed emotion. Shawn wrote about these techniques in the book, *Every Little Movement*.

Ted Shawn, 1891–1972

Shawn taught baseball, football, and basketball players, wrestlers, and track stars dances with strong masculine themes such as *Olympiad* and *Labor Symphony*. Through his efforts, he helped to raise the status of the male dancer in the United States by choreographing themes that promoted the masculine characteristics of the dancers.

Another major contribution to the dance world by Ted Shawn has been the founding of the Jacob's Pillow center in Massachusetts. This is a residence for dancers where they may study and perform. A festival is held there late each summer when works are presented in concert.

Mary Wigman, who came from the German School of modern dance, was another influential pioneer. Wigman was regarded as the genius and the leader of German modern dance from 1924. She studied dance with Dalcroze (whose full name was Émile Jaques-Dalcroze and who created a way to teach the coordination of music and body movements called *eurythmics*) and with Rudolf Laban (who

Mary Wigman, 1886–1973

developed one of the methods of recording body movements on paper, which is now called *Labanotation*).

Because she was concerned with self-expression, Wigman's contributions included psychological and emotional approaches to creativity. She felt that dance should be movement alone, so she composed dances without music. She fully explored the use of space. Her dances were described as "stark, primordial, harsh, gloomy, preoccupied with death." Wigman visited the United States in the early 1930s and again in 1964.

Hanya Holm, 1898–

Wigman's pupil, Hanya Holm, adapted the German modern dance to the needs and characteristics of American dancers. As a master teacher of modern dance, she influenced many dancers with her concepts of space. Holm was one of the few modern dance choreographers also successful as a choreographer for the Broadway musical stage. Her most famous musical was "My Fair Lady."

Martha Graham, 1894–

Probably the most exacting technique and the greatest number of choreographic works have come from Martha Graham. Her technique is built on the breathing cycle of the body and its principle of "contraction and release." (Other principles developed by her are called "motor memory" and "percussive movement.") In brief, Graham's dance is built on the process of inhaling and exhaling. She believes that in inhaling the body has an aerial quality of release, and in exhaling the body "drive has gone down and out" in contraction. Many of today's dancers, choreographers, and modern dance classes have been influenced by her technique.

Another major contribution by Miss Graham has been in the area of choreography and performance. She was considered one of the finest dance concert performers. She utilized the wide spectrum of life in the themes of her outstanding works. She often used themes from Greek drama to symbolize and probe the inner man. Her dance company has included some of the outstanding dancers in the world.

Doris Humphrey, 1895–1958

Martha Graham and Doris Humphrey both left Denishawn, and each established her own school. Both developed theories and philosophies of movement that are significant to the growth of modern dance, and both are considered to be in the art's third generation.

Doris Humphrey was a protégé of Ruth St. Denis and her movements were of the same lyrical quality. She built her dance principles on the "fall-recovery" theory which she created. She believed dance movement came about by periods of unbalance and balance in the body. She stated that "fall-recovery" consisted of three separate movements: the *fall*, the *recovery* from the fall, and the *suspension* held at the peak of recovery. She also perfected compositions using large-scale dramatic themes for groups of dancers.

She formed an alliance with Charles Weidman, who had also been in the Denishawn Company. Weidman is known for his biting, satirical dance works and his skill as a performer. Together they formed one branch of American modern dance. Miss Humphrey performed her works until 1945, when crippling arthritis ended her performing career. She continued choreographing and working until her death.

Charles Weidman, 1901–1975

Some of her most brilliant works from 1945 on were created for José Limón, an important choreographer in his own right. His powerful body and magnificent carriage and bearing always marked his strong masculine performances. He formed his own company in 1946 and continued to choreograph dramatic works until his death.

José Limón, 1908–1972

Of the dancers who worked in the 1960s, Merce Cunningham stirred the most controversy with his works. Cunningham choreographs "by chance," holding to the idea that "any movement can follow any other movement." Regarded as avant-garde, he has choreographed and performed works that audiences either adore or abhor, depending upon their individual convictions. His admirers point to his fine artistic sense, his intelligence, and his superb company as factors that make the works he creates brilliant movement pieces. Cunningham has maintained a long artistic collaboration with composer John Cage, who is known for his philosophy that all sound could be regarded as music. Their collaboration has produced works that have created new artistic realms.

Merce Cunningham, 1919–

Alwin Nikolais is another American modern dance choreographer. His contribution has been in the creation of a form of theater that includes props, costumes, films, slides, sound, and light as extensions of the bodies of the dancers. His visual effects and illusions often remind the audience of events in their own experience, yet the works contain no story or conventional plot. The dancers' bodies are often distorted or hidden in the costumes and props to emphasize Nikolais' abstract images and suggestions.

Alwin Nikolais, 1912–

Anna Sokolow, 1912– Another reknowned choreographer is Anna Sokolow, whose powerful social statements characterize her works. Her commitment to the socialist movement, evident in her early works, gave way as time progressed to a more general concern with the feelings and problems of all humanity. Sokolow has used many different types of music, including jazz, and has choreographed extensively in Mexico and Israel as well as in the United States.

Alvin Ailey, 1931– Many modern dancers have contributed to the development of modern dance as an art in America. Alvin Ailey's great gift is his ability to present exciting, theatrical pieces that reflect the black experience. His first company was composed of all black dancers, but now all races of dancers perform works by many different choreographers. The present repertory company performs works aimed at a combination of art and entertainment. The company is very popular and tours regularly.

Paul Taylor, 1930– Paul Taylor also has taken modern dance to new artistic levels. Taylor danced with Graham and Cunningham but has developed a style that is definitely his own. He is known for his choreographic wit, logical placings of movements, groupings of dancers, and satire. He has also created pieces cleverly repeating a limited number of movements over and over again in unusual ways. He has not performed since 1974 but still choreographs for his company extensively.

Bella Lewitzky, 1916– Bella Lewitzky is unique to the world of modern dance because she made her reputation as an artist in California instead of New York. Not since Denishawn had a modern dance choreographer of major importance become established anywhere but in New York. Like Alvin Ailey, she was trained in California by Lester Horton (who died in 1958). Her choreography is known for its powerful images and for extensive use of space, isolations, and quick movements. Lewitzky is also known for her extraordinary ability as a performing artist.

During the 1960s modern dance reflected the social and political unrest that pervaded the decade. Many changes occurred. The only consistent characteristic was a discarding of the idea of theatricality and use of everyday, pedestrian movement. Some dancers and choreographers were saying "no" to the idea of modern dance as it then existed.

Many times traditional leotards, tights, and theatrical costumes were discarded for such utilitarian garments as overalls and hard hats, gym shorts and tennis shoes, sweat shirts and jeans—or even nudity. The 1960s and 1970s produced new names for modern dance, including anti-dance, non-dance, minimal dance, environmental dance, dance without walls, verbal dance, and alternate space dance. Dance was sometimes performed in such nontraditional spaces as museums, malls, parking lots, parks, streets, and country clubs. Such spaces change the way dance is performed. And many times the dance is directed and choreographed by a dancer but performed by dancers and nondancers alike.

These periods of fertile creativity were characterized by a fresh look at time, space, and sound. Much of the movement was anti-proscenium theater in which ordinary movement, by ordinary people, in ordinary places was considered valid as art. Many dancers collaborated on an equal basis with composers and studio artists to make pieces, or "events," as they were sometimes called. Before this generation of dancers, choreographers gave ideas to a composer or designer and then waited for the results. Now the collaboration often took place simultaneously with all of the artists contributing to the work.

As the decade of the 1970s drew to a close, two distinct camps of modern dance existed. One camp became more and more technically oriented and produced dances that were more and more difficult to perform. Dancers needed to study for periods of time with a choreographer to develop the style and technique needed to perform that choreographer's works. These choreographers followed more directly the established artists of the generation who had preceded them. They did not necessarily create in the same way as their teachers had, but they used many of the preceding generation's methods and ideas to create their own original works. Some of the artists involved with the more theatrically motivated modern dance are Murray Lewis, Jennifer Mueller, Bill Evans, Cliff Keuter, Twyla Tharp, Lar Lubovitch, Gloria Newman, and Pilobolus.

Another camp became more and more anti-dance. Time, space, and energy were altered to make new forms, meanings, and nonmeanings in the modern dance. Most of these choreographers had also studied and worked with the preceding generation of choreographers, but they discarded many of that generation's ideas to do new, different, exciting things in dance. A few of the artists involved with this camp of modern dance in the 1970s were Don Redlich, Rudy Perez, Yvonne Rainer, Meredith Monk, Kei Taikei, Anna Halprin, and Douglas Dunn.

As dancers and choreographers explore new ways of moving and create more relevant means of communication with the audience, modern dance changes, incorporates, and adopts these new ideas. The difference between the pioneers and the dancers of today is that today's dancers have a strong, proven foundation from which to work. Modern dance has only one predictable characteristic: it is always changing and growing. This is the trait that makes it exciting and significant.

Choreographic Approaches

Chapter 6

*Each dance is unique and free, a separate organism
whose form is self-determined.*

— Mary Wigman

Some students ask, "Why should I study choreography when all I want to do is dance?" It's true that a brilliant dancer may never have choreographed anything, and a brilliant choreographer may have been a poor dancer. A successful performer, however, doesn't just dance. You dance about something or to express something, even when the dance is without a plot. If you hope to make a statement with your body that reflects your intentions or the choreographer's, you should have some idea of the choreographic structure behind the dance you are doing. If you want to teach dancing or choreograph someday, then you can save yourself countless hours of aimless experimentation by knowing a few techniques of how to begin your experiments.

Improvisation and basic choreographic forms should be as much a part of your training as daily technique classes. Technique classes train the body. Improvisation frees your movement from the restrictions placed on it by a codified technique and frees your own creative energies. Knowledge of choreographic structures train your mind and sharpens your critical faculties and perceptions.

There are many ways to choreograph. You will find the way that works best for you. We have presented here only a few basic approaches to choreographic exploration.

A sense of body design in space and good stage balance comes with experience. You can do a number of things to

DESIGN

55

Observing Design

help develop your "artistic eye" for line, form shape, and theatrical drama.

Pictures are telegraphic. They tell you a story without the addition of a caption below them. Dance should be able to do the same. Try the following exercises to help develop your artistic eye: (1) Look at paintings of different periods of history. Observe how the artist has placed the people in relationship to one another, how the people are posed, and why their clothes make them stand out the way they do. (2) Study the pictures in a pictorial magazine like *Life* and see why some pictures and advertisements hold your attention. (3) Look at the pictures of athletes in "frozen" motion and trace the natural lines of their movement. (4) Look at the buildings or the landscape around you and ask what is beautiful, interesting, or jarring about it.

Study people and nature. If you want to dance about people and their universal concerns, you have to understand them and what makes them behave as they do in a given set of circumstances. (1) Watch how people of different ages and social classes walk, sit, and stand. (2) Observe how people move when they are happy, sad, or expressing some emotion. (3) Watch how people in a social situation group themselves into a circle or how some sit off by themselves. (4) Watch how children, animals, and birds move and consider why they move that way. (5) Study the shapes formed by a tree, a leaf, a rock, or oil stains on a mud puddle. (6) Become acutely aware of your own senses. How do different textures feel? Be aware of odors; notice the taste of your food; really study how something looks, its shapes, its colors; and start to listen carefully to the sounds of nature and to man-made sounds. (7) Begin to notice natural movements, such as the sway of trees, the ebb and flow of waves, or the ripples in a pond. Try to sense the dynamics of the motion and how your body could suggest that movement and its dynamics.

All of life, all of nature, is potentially the concern of the artist who must bring some kind of order out of the myriad possibilities through selection and emphasis. Basically choreography can be thought of as planning movement of the human body through space and time. It requires choices in body movement and spatial design, rate of speed, rhythm, dynamics, and overall form. To have merit the materials of dance need to be manipulated imaginatively rather than as a series of movements strung together without coherence. Developing appropriate movements takes time and discipline.

Choreographers work in many different ways, some letting the dance shape itself, others having clearly established ideas they wish to communicate. For the beginning choreographer it is usually helpful to define the theme of your study or work. It is helpful to consider what the content of the study will be, its logical development, what it will communicate. All sections should flow naturally into one another and have coherence to the whole.

There are two basic modes of stage design: symmetrical and asymmetrical. In symmetrical design the stage is equally balanced on both sides. For example, if you have two dancers on one side of the stage, then you have two dancers on the other side. In asymmetrical design, the stage is not balanced. *Two Kinds of Design*

 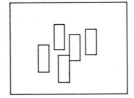

If you have two dancers on one side of the stage, you might have four on the other side in staggered positions. Symmetrical design is the most pleasing to look at, but it becomes the dullest to look at if overused. Another kind of design is dynamic design achieved by linear spacing of dancers or massed grouping; the first establishes the line, the second a sense of volume or mass.

Presumably you are choreographing for an audience, so you want to keep their eyes constantly "entertained" with unexpected movements, lines, shapes, and forms. There is nothing worse than putting your audience to sleep. There are no bad audiences—only bad dancers and choreographers. You have a responsibility to communicate something to a paying audience even if it is outraged at what you have done. The worst thing you can do to your audience is cause indifference or boredom, unless that is your intention.

Where does movement originate? An important primary source is yourself. Under the direction of your teacher, improvisation is an effective method to begin the develop- *IMPROVISATION* ment of your own movement style. If you involve yourself in the spirit of improvisation, eventually you will find the way of moving that "feels right" for your body, based on all you have experienced in life. Through suggestions, your teacher can help you find the way of moving that is unique because it originates from you and you alone.

Your teacher will have a particular way of conducting improvisations. Some teachers incorporate them into a technique class, others include them in a separate composition class or some other format. In beginning improvisation some dancers feel shy or embarrassed about moving freely in front of others in the class. This feeling can be overcome. The sooner it is overcome, the more pleasures and rewards will result from the experience.

When your teacher gives you directions for an improvisation, listen carefully. When you are ready to begin, do not plan your movements ahead of time. Let them flow naturally based on the instructions given. Try to stay within the structure outlined. Avoid trying to imitate some movement sequence you have seen or learned elsewhere. Try to let things happen naturally without forcing them to happen. Don't be concerned about how the movement looks to others who might be watching. Concentrate on what you are doing. Remember that this is your own movement experience and that later your teacher can give you helpful suggestions. The more you improvise, the easier it becomes.

Following are some improvisational exercises that may supplement the work given in the classroom. Try to do them when you are alone. Allow yourself plenty of time with each part of an exercise so that you don't feel rushed. Don't feel that you have to accomplish something, because there are no right or wrong results.

Exercises   The first two exercises may help you get in touch with your own body, body weight, and body rhythm.

1. Start lying on the floor. Take some time to sense your body. Are there any tensions anywhere? Stretch your body from head to foot, open the arms and legs wide to the side, then relax. Repeat several times. Try to get a sense of what is happening in the body as you stretch and relax. Next, be aware of the shape of your body and how each part relates to the other parts of your body. Move to new positions of lying and again note the changing body shape and the relationship of the body parts.

Next, lying on your back, be aware of each part of your body in contact with the floor. Be aware of the weight of your body. Slowly lift and then lower various parts of your body, for example, an arm, a leg, and parts of the torso. Be aware of the weight of the body part and the kind of energy required to lift and lower it. Next, to sense your breath rhythms and how the body lengthens and widens in space, take a few moments to concentrate on how your body moves when you inhale and exhale. Without forcing, lengthen your body from the top of the head to the toes as you inhale, and shorten your body from the head to the toes as you exhale. Repeat this a number of times, and then vary the idea by widening your body as you inhale and narrowing your body as you exhale.

Next, to get a sense of your own rhythm, gently roll each part of your body from side to side on the floor—the head, a leg, an arm, the torso, and so forth. Be aware of the sensation of the movement and your body in contact with the floor. Next, gently roll the whole body from side to side and eventually roll over like a log being rolled. Next, to get a sense of your body weight working with gravity, again start by being aware of your breathing. As you inhale lift your head off the floor and as you exhale lower the head to the floor. Without straining as you inhale, lift the torso off the floor and as you exhale let the movement subside onto the floor. Continue this rising and lowering, rising higher with each inhalation until you come to a standing position.

2. Standing up, try to be free of any unnecessary tension in your body. Stand as still as possible and try to determine if there is any subtle, involuntary motion taking place in your body in response to the demands of standing upright. Try the same thing standing on both feet with eyes closed, standing on one foot, and standing on the balls of the feet. Next, again be aware of your breathing. Without forcing, lengthen your body upward as you inhale, and lower your body as you exhale. Next, as you inhale rise to the balls of your feet and stretch your arms overhead; as you exhale fall forward and catch your weight on one foot.

Return to the starting position and repeat the action, falling to each side and to the back. Repeat again. Make certain the whole body is involved, and note the kind of energy you are using as you rise, fall, and recover. Repeat the action again with a rhythm of some kind, for example, rise, fall, recover, pause—rise, fall, recover, pause. Next, try varying the rhythm, for example, rise-rise-rise (slow), fall (fast), recover (fast) or rise (fast), fall-fall-fall (slow), recover (fast). The rate of the speed may change the dynamics or quality of the movement. If so, try to sense how your body adapts to the changing dynamics.

3. The next exercise may help you get a sense of the space around your body and how you can move through it. Stand quietly and visualize all the space around your body in front, in back, to the sides, above, and below you. Imagine that the space has the consistency of the sculptor's modeling clay. From every direction gather the space into yourself. Then mold or give shape to the imaginary clay—for example, various sizes of spheres, cubes, and so forth. Clearly indicate the size and weight of the molded object. Be aware of the rhythm of your actions as you knead, shape, pat, and smooth the "clay." Next, tear the molded space into small pellets and hurl them or scatter them individually in every direction around your body.

Next, try scattering or throwing imaginary objects, for example, a feather, a leaf, a marble, a shotput, a coin, or a piece of paper. Be aware of the kind of energy required in order to throw each object. Next, imagine how each object would move through space and settle to the ground. Imagining your body as the thrown object, try to move and settle the same way. Involve the whole body and make the movements as broad as possible. This exercise should help you to avoid making fragmented movements.

4. This exercise may help you to develop a movement phrase. Select one word from each of the lists below and write the eight words sequentially on paper. Without preplanning, move your whole body in the way the eight-word description suggests. Keep repeating the sequence until you have a phrase that feels natural to you and that seems to have a beginning, a middle, and an end.

Next try the same phrase by moving in a way that would be opposite to the original descriptive word. If the word is *fast*, for example, move slowly. Now replace the first and next-to-last words of your list with two more words from one of the eight categories. Let the first word be the beginning of your phrase and the next-to-last word be the ending. When you have established three movement phrases, try to give each one a beginning, a conclusion, and a transition into the next sequence. Decide whether any of the movements could be enriched by being performed another way, whether some movements ought to be eliminated or repeated a number of times. "Editing" one's work is an important function for the choreographer. Movements must be discarded if they do not contribute to the whole phrase or theme.

TIME	BODY SHAPE	MOVEMENT DIRECTION	FLOOR PATTERN
slow	spread out	over	dodge
very slow	closed in	under	zigzag
fast	large	through	jagged
very fast	small	across	drift
slow-fast	tall	open out	circle
fast-slow	short	toward	spiral in
sustained	curved	away	spiral out
sudden	angular	rise	wavelike
leisurely	thin	sink	straight
rushed	stout	side	diagonal
held back	growing	diagonal	square
held	diminishing	around	triangle

IMAGE	ACTION	ACTION	STARTING POSITION IN ROOM
melting	crouch	pull	center
floating	throw	press	front of center
jerky	catch	strike	back of center
bumpy	crawl	slash	left of center
bubbling	drop	dab	left front
pulsating	swing	flick	left back
smooth	rock	pound	right of center
percussive	turn	shake	right front
light	bounce	squeeze	right back
heavy	jump	wring	
free	stretch	glide	
restrained	twist	touch	

Emotions, ideas, images, and atmosphere can be used separately or together, or they can be combined with other approaches. Here are examples of their use together: (1) Imagine yourself in a room full of strangers on a hot, humid day. Thread your way through the room without touching

Emotions, Ideas, Images, and Atmosphere

the people. Exaggerate the adjustments your body makes to avoid contact. (2) Imagine yourself in a brightly lit room. Suddenly the lights go out; you hear strange noises that you finally realize are made by the walls closing in on you. The walls close in until they have forced you into a tiny ball on the floor. Express your reactions to these events with movements as exaggerated as you can make them. (3) Move your whole body broadly through some everyday actions such as brushing your teeth, sewing, clipping your nails, brushing your hair, or twisting the cap off a bottle. (4) Crouch on the floor, making yourself as small as possible. Then slowly unfold your body and spread out in every direction until you fill the entire room. Now reverse the action. Repeat the sequence with a sense of joy as you rise and a sense of grief as you descend. Repeat again, rising like a roaring brush fire and descending as if your body had turned to liquid. (5) Remember how you felt this morning when you got out of bed. Walking around the room, try to get the same feeling in your movements. Exaggerate the movements and sustain the mood as you walk freely around the room.

MOTIVE AND CHARACTER Another approach to finding new movement or to defining a character in a dance work is to improvise from human stereotypes, from the psychological make-up of a specific person, from gestures or common movement activities like throwing a ball, or by using an animal as a reference point for character definition.

If you are going to choreograph a part—a swaggering braggart, for example—you could ask yourself such questions as what motivates this person, what does he want, and how does he move. An easy way to begin is to decide that he acts like some animal, maybe a strutting rooster. You could then improvise around the idea of a rooster strutting with his chest pushed forward and his head quickly surveying all of his domain.

Gesture Another approach to defining his character with movement is to improvise on some imaginary situation he might be in. For example, if he were in a room full of people and was offered food, how would he take the food from a tray and how would he eat it?

If the movement is to be repeated and set into a dance for the character, it is helpful to decide first on a few extreme examples of what this person moves like, or extreme static poses that he might assume, then combine them to-gether, moving from static positions or from movement pattern to movement pattern. You can eventually arrive at specific movements that get your idea across. The tendency with novice choreographers is to put everything they know indiscriminately into the dance. An audience will probably see the choreography only once and so must be carefully led to see the idea that you want them to see.

You will not always choreograph or dance as a literal, recognizable character, but sometimes as an abstraction of an idea or character. These same methods of choreographic improvisation and definition can be utilized until you have arrived at the essence of what you wanted to say in move-ment. For example, if you pick a flower from a garden, you could go through the actual motions of picking a flower (literal gesture) or a stylized motion of picking a flower (pantomime) or an extended motion suggesting the picking of a flower, indicating the joy or nostalgia you feel, rather than the actual picking of the flower (dance). *Abstraction of Character*

Many people have ideas but lack the ability to share them with others. That is why you as a choreographer or dancer have to develop the craft of organizing your ideas into some structure that will communicate them to the audience. *FORMS*

There is no easy formula that will guarantee success, but a few forms that you can organize your ideas around are presented here as possibilities to start with. (Some of these basic forms require more than one dancer.)

The theme is one of the most elemental forms. It is par-ticularly useful when you begin to choreograph extended pieces. A theme makes some basic statement and is or-ganized around some central movement idea. For example, using the idea of a "work theme" you could choreograph a movement pattern of eight bars suggesting the movements of a lumberman chopping down a tree. The movement theme: he chops the tree. *Theme*

The basic movement theme is shown once, then repeated with some kind of basic change. The common ways of doing the variation are: (1) Slowing down or (2) speeding up the entire movement pattern; (3) inverting the movement (for example, movements that go up now go down, movements that came toward the body now go away from the body); (4) reversing the movement pattern (that is, starting at the *Theme and Variation* end and working toward the beginning); (5) extending the amount of time selected movements are performed or (6) diminishing the amount of time selected movements are performed; and (7) embellishing or adding movement to the basic theme or (8) eliminating movement from the basic theme.

Starting with the basic chopping theme, then doing each of these eight variations for eight bars, you would end up with a choreographic piece that was seventy-two bars long. In embellishing the basic theme you might add the idea that the lumberman stops to wipe his brow with a handkerchief because of the heat or he stops to sharpen the cutting blade or to watch the tree fall.

By combining the basic theme with variations or with some other form, you can tell a story or suggest a change of mood or anything that you want to communicate, and yet beneath it all is a basic structure that has a unity with your basic premise, the original eight bars of movement.

A.B.A.   Another common form is A.B.A.—the statement of a basic theme (A), a second theme (B), and a repetition of the original theme (A). The lumberman is chopping briskly with a steady rhythm in the first theme; in the second theme he tires, and the chopping slows down and changes rhythm frequently; then he gets a "second wind" and again chops briskly with a steady rhythm.

Fugue   The fugue requires more than one dancer. For example, you start with a basic theme of chopping for eight bars. This original eight bars is repeated exactly the same way by the same dancer or other dancers throughout the entire piece, while the original dancer or some other dancer(s) does variations on the original theme.

Sonata   The sonata form is made up of two themes, primary and secondary, plus a recapitulation or joining of the two themes. For example, in theme one the man chops the tree. In theme two the man watches the tree fall. In the recapitulation the man again chops the tree and watches it fall. In such a re-capitulation of the two themes you might have the idea of felling a forest and not merely one tree.

Round   The round is a common form exemplified by the song "Three Blind Mice." The same theme is repeated a number of times with new dancers joining in at some point. The beginning dancer finishes first, then the other dancers stop as they finish the same movement pattern. For example, (movement A) the man chops the tree, (movement B) the man wipes his brow, and (movement C) the man watches the tree fall. In a simple round the first dancer(s) starts at movement A, continues through movements B and C, and stops. The second dancer(s) begins at movement A when the first dancer begins movement B and continues to the end and stops. The third dancer(s) begins movement A when the second dancer begins at movement B and continues to the end and stops. The first dancer, instead of stopping at the end of movement C, may introduce new movement themes which are repeated by the second and third dancer.

The canon form is similar to the round except that all *Canon* the dancers finally join in the same movement to bring it to an end (coda). In dance canon, each new dancer does the movement exactly as the original movement was done, but the new dancer may be a different physical or emotional type from the original dancer. In the original theme the lumberman chops the tree. In the successive repeats of the theme he may be joined by his wife and then by his son.

In counterpoint two independent themes are danced *Counterpoint* against one another. The lumberman chops the tree while someone builds a house using the material the lumberman has produced.

Choreography by chance is here called a form because the *Chance* artist must still select and shape the final piece. A common *Composition* example might be your placing a certain number of move-ment instructions written on individual pieces of paper into a box, then drawing them out one at a time and assembling them into a movement pattern in the same order you drew them out. For example, you might draw out these instruc-tions (1) move in a circle, (2) make percussive movements, and (3) exhale. Using the idea of the lumberman, you might have him circle the tree, chop it sharply, and exhale with fatigue. It should be understood, however, that choreog-raphy by chance usually implies the lack of a preconceived theme.

All of these forms could, of course, be built around some other theme—abstract, literal, or movement-oriented.

Music can add a great deal to your choreography or it can *MUSIC* destroy it. There are a few things to keep in mind when you are working with music. (However, you might want to choreograph the dance in *opposition* to these ideas in order to achieve a dissonant look in your movement.) (1) Keep the qualities of the dance movement consistent with the mood of the music (or, for contrast, deliberately work against the mood of the music). (2) Analyze the structure of the music so that you can repeat the movements on the same counts or phrases twice running or so that you can teach the movement to someone else without being vague about what happens when. A pencil and paper are invaluable. Makes dashes on the paper in accompaniment with the regular beats of the music until you have developed some kind of musical pattern to work from. As you listen over and over to the music, make notes above the dashes to indicate shifts in the rhythm, shifts in the mood, or new instruments entering—or make whatever other notes can guide you. (3) Try composing your own music. You might play it *while you are dancing* or have someone play it for you. You can use percussion instruments if they are available. If not, so much the better: find and use rocks, sticks, or dried leaves on a branch. Or run a comb over paper. You can discover exciting new sounds by trying out the unlikeliest objects. Then organize the sounds into some repeatable form. If you have access to a tape recorder, you can record your music. A tape recorder makes it possible to use other sounds as well, like a ticking clock, an airplane, dripping water, or a cat's cry. Composing your own music frees you from the restrictions placed on you by the composer, and can be a lot of fun as well.

COSTUMES, PROPS, AND SCENERY

If you are going to wear a costume or use scenery and props, take advantage of them by analyzing their function in relation to your purposes. For example, if you are wearing a long cape, experiment to find out how many different ways you can move it or use it to augment the spatial designs of your body. Can it be used as a prop like a bullfighter's cape or placed on the floor to suggest a forbidden territory that no one dares enter? The important thing to remember about a dance costume is that you don't just wear it, you take advantage of its restrictions and use them to enhance your visual designs or enhance your ideas.

Costumes do not need to be expensive in order to be effective. Using your leotards and tights as a basic costume, you can perform wonders with pieces of unsewn material or dyes.

If you use stage props, explore all their possibilities. For example, an ordinary chair can be sat on, lain on, stood on, crawled under or over, or danced with like a silent partner. The list is endless.

Costumes, props, and scenery make it possible to extend the potentials of your body design in space and to add new elements of stage interest. The only limitations to movement possibilities are those that come from your not being imaginative or from your deliberately being selective.

If you become discouraged in your experiments, keep in mind that even the most famous of choreographers started at the beginning. No less than they, you have to work at your craft if you want eventually to use it to express your ideas and feelings.

Evaluation and Criticism

Chapter 7

We have to meet the artist halfway. We have to bring something before we can bring something away.
— Clive Barnes

Often you hear people say of something they have seen, "I liked it," or "I didn't like it." This is the beginning of criticism. Unfortunately most people never go beyond these statements to analyze why they "liked" or "didn't like" what they saw.

If you want to dance, choreograph, teach, or be an intelligent member of the audience, it is important to you that you know why you "liked" or "didn't like" something and be able to express your viewpoint intelligently. You can learn a great deal of what to do and what not to do in the dance theater by seeing dance concerts and by critically evaluating what you have seen. Your criticisms should never be exclusively negative or positive. You should impartially evaluate both the good and the bad features.

You may not be able to see dance concerts regularly, but you can increase your critical faculties and perceptions in other ways. Every movie, television show, advertisement, short story, etc., has a structure and makes a statement in some way—good or bad. You can apply the same principles to these communication forms that you do to dance. Each time you see a dance work, you are increasing your ability to judge and critique a dance.

You can analyze the overall structure by asking yourself how it began, how it ended, and what happened in between. A well-structured dance should have a beginning, a development of the beginning, and a resolution. The form may or may not be used to tell a story. Nevertheless, it should start somewhere, accomplish something, and be resolved.

With a professional company you have the right to ask if the work was performed well and if the dancers contributed to the choreographer's conception. Many good works are ruined by bad dancers, and many bad works are effective when performed by good dancers. Was it theatrically exciting? There is no law that says art cannot be entertaining. The audience has a right to expect something more for its time and money than a pedestrian presentation of an idea.

The following lists give you some ideas to increase your critical and evaluative skills and to consider when doing your own choreography.

1. Was there a unifying theme that could be identified? *THE DANCE AS*
2. Did the theme of the work have relevance to you? Was *A WHOLE* the theme portrayed adequately? Could you understand the theme and its importance to the choreographer?
3. What was your idea of what the dance was about? Did it correspond to program notes and to the title of the piece? Did the title adequately reflect the idea of the work?
4. Did the spatial patterns provide conceptual movements that promoted the theme? Whether the patterns contrast or complement does not matter—the aesthetic feel of the patterns is what counts.
5. Did the floor patterns contribute to the idea of the dance? Whether the patterns are varied or repetitive, they must promote the theme.
6. Was the element of time correct for the work? The movement may be fast, slow, medium, or a combination thereof, but time must fit the concept of the piece.
7. Was there an element of surprise, tension, humor, or drama? Were any of these really necessary?
8. Was there one outstanding moment you can remember?
9. Was there a beginning, middle, and end? Were these necessary?
10. Did the work challenge you to think in terms of a new concept or time, energy, space, or dance?
11. Did the choreographer introduce a concept of performance that was different from what you had previously experienced?

12. Did the work succeed?
13. Would you like to see the performance again?
14. Were the individual movements and movement patterns original and visually interesting as well as logically related to the whole work?

Technical Considerations

1. Did the technical support generally enhance the performance?
2. Did the music, sound, words, or silence enhance the theme? Was the sound too large or too small for the work? Was the music chopped and rearranged so as to distort the composer's purpose?
3. Was the lighting design and execution suitable for the piece? Was it too dark to see the dancer? Did the lights overpower the movement?
4. Did the costumes contribute to or detract from the piece? Could a change of costume give an added dimension? Were the costumes manipulated well? Did they flatter the dancers' bodies?
5. Were the props an integral part of the work? Were they used in an imaginative manner? Did the dancers seem at ease with them?
6. Were the make-up and hair designs appropriate for the dance?

Performance Considerations

1. Were the dancers well trained for what they were asked to perform?
2. Did the dancers work well together during the performance?
3. Was the number of dancers correct for the piece?
4. Were the dancers involved with projecting the idea of the work rather than with their technique or their bodies?
5. Did the dancers seem to be well rehearsed?
6. Did the dancers seem secure and at ease with the movement and the piece?

You may or may not like the performance, but you should be able to understand the choreographer's ideas and to appreciate the way the ideas were created and developed. If you didn't like it, ask yourself first if you came with a preconception of what dance is supposed to be, and this company didn't live up to your idea. If you want to develop your critical abilities and sensibilities, you have to be open to new ideas and new approaches in dance. Remember that many of the dance movements of the modern dance pioneers were thought strange and ugly by an audience unaccustomed to this new way of moving.

Many times the old rules do not readily apply to a work you have seen. Remember the established methods and rules of choreography and performance are merely a foundation to be built upon. New ideas are constantly being created and developed. Some dances are composed to be anti-theatrical, and some are performed in spaces other than a traditional theater or proscenium stage. For these reasons alone, the shape and content of modern dance keeps changing. You don't have to accept as "great" everything you see, but you should know why you consider something great, mediocre, or merely pleasing.

Like the muscles of your body, your critical faculties and perceptions are developed by being used regularly. Incorrect training makes muscles that are undesirably bulky. In a similar way, a closed mind impedes your creativity and stops the flow of new ideas in your evaluations and in your own work.

ℰelected References

Preparation   De Mille, Agnes. *To a Young Dancer.* Boston and Toronto: Little, Brown, 1962.

Reynolds, Nancy, (ed.). *The Dance Catalogue: A Complete Guide to Today's World of Dance.* New York: Harmony Books, Crown, 1979.

Terry, Walter. *Careers for the 70's Dance.* New York: Crowell-Collier, 1971.

Anatomy   Arnheim, Daniel D., and Joan Schlaich. *Dance Injuries: Their Prevention and Care.* St. Louis, Mo.: Mosby, 1975.

Gelabert, Raoul. *Anatomy for the Dancer,* 2 vols. New York: Dance Magazine, 1964 and 1966.

Vincent, Larry. *Dancer's Book of Health.* Mission, Kansas: Sheed, Andrews, & McMeel, 1978.

History   McDonagh, Don. *The Complete Guide to Modern Dance.* Garden City, New Jersey: Doubleday, 1976.

————. *The Rise and Fall and Rise of Modern Dance.* New York: Outerbridge and Dienstfrey, 1970.

Martin, John. *Introduction to the Dance.* Brooklyn: Dance Horizons, 1965.

Mazo, Joseph H. *Prime Movers: The Makers of Modern Dance in America.* New York: William Morrow, 1977.

Choreography   Cunningham, Merce. *Changes: Notes on Choreography.* New York: Something Else, 1968.

Ellfeldt, Lois. *A Primer for Choreographers.* Palo Alto, Calif.; National Press, 1967.

Humphrey, Doris. *The Art of Making Dances.* New York: Grove, 1959.

Smith, Jacqueline. *Dance Composition: A Practical Guide for Teachers.* Old Working, Surrey: Lepus Books, 1976.

Croce, Arlene. *Afterimages.* New York: Alfred A. Knopf, 1978. *Evaluation and Criticism*

Jowitt, Deborah. *Dance Beat: Selected Views and Reviews, 1967– 1976.* New York: Marcel Dekker, 1977.

Siegel, Marcia B. *Watching the Dance Go By.* New York: Houghton Mifflin, 1977.

Mueller, John. *Dance Film Directory: An Annotated and Evalua- Films tive Guide to Films on Ballet and Modern Dance.* Princeton, N.J.: Princeton Books, 1979.

Cage, John. *Silence.* Middletown, Conn.: Wesleyan University, Miscellaneous 1961.

Cohen, Selma Jean. *The Modern Dance: Seven Statements of Belief.* Middletown, Conn.: Wesleyan University, 1966.

Laban, Rudolf. *Modern Educational Dance.* London: MacDonald and Evans, 1948.

Dance Magazine (published monthly). 10 Columbus Circle, New York, New York 10019.

Dance Scope (published quarterly). 152 West 42nd Street, New York, New York 10036.

Index

Clockwise from upper left: Alwin
Nikolais (photo by Basil Langton),
Anna Sokolow, Merce Cunningham
(photo by Gerda Peterich, from The
Library & Museum of the Performing
Arts, The New York Public Library at
Lincoln Center), Alvin Ailey (photo by
Bob Greene/The Alvin Ailey American
Dance Theater), Paul Taylor (The Paul
Taylor Dance Foundation, Inc.), and
Bella Lewitzky (photo by Lynn Smith/
Bella Lewitzky Dance Company)